DESIGNING TO DECO...
A STEP BY STEP GUIDE TO CREATING BEAUTIFUL R...

John Payne
Miniature Mansions

Published in the United Kingdom by:-

Deacon publications

Content copyright © John Payne 2017

Photography, layout and illustrations copyright © 2017

All rights reserved. No portion of this book may be reproduced, stored in a retrieval system or transmitted at any time or by any means, without the prior permission in writing of John Payne or as expressly permitted by law.

The designs in this book are copyright and must not be made for resale.

The right of John Payne to be identified as the author of this work has been asserted by him in accordance with the Copyright, Design and Patents Act 1988.

A CIP record of this book is available from the British Library.

First published in the UK in 2017

ISBN 978-1-5262-0675-6

Photography by Delmar Studio.

Edited by Eleanor Ayres.

Book Design John Payne.

Printed by Acanthus Press for Deacon Publications.

The step by step guides in this book **are not** suitable for children.

Contents

FOREWORD	2
PREFACE	2
INTRODUCTION	3
CHAPTER 1	5
Tools	
CHAPTER 2	10
Making templates	
Drawing the design	
CHAPTER 3	21
Preparation of mouldings	
Painting walls	
Wallpapering	
CHAPTER 4	29
Decorating a ceiling	
CHAPTER 5	34
Wall design	
CHAPTER 6	37
The Knowledge	
CHAPTER 7	62
Templates	

FOREWORD

Miniature Mansions provides the ambitious doll's house maker with a very useful range of decorative mouldings. Now John Payne has written a clear, no-nonsense guide to using them that took me right back to my Woodwork for Beginners class at the local adult college in the late 1970s, before the London Dollshouse Festival at Kensington Town Hall (which we started in 1985) was even a twinkle in my eye.

The steady growth of good craftsmanship in miniatures and the passionate ambition of so many collectors to house them as grandly as possible, has led to a steady growth in useful materials in the mini-building industry, but many novices still need basic help to get going and here they have it.

Caroline Hamilton

Author of *Decorative Dolls' Houses* (1990) and co-author with Jane Fiddick of *Our Dollshouses* at Newby Hall in North Yorkshire where our joint collections are on permanent (but seasonal) display since 2015.

PREFACE

In writing this book I hope to pass on some of the skills, techniques and knowledge I have gained over the past 40 years as a model maker. I have worked in most disciplines from architectural models to product prototypes and models for films.

I was fortunate to learn my craft at Piper Models, one of London's top architectural model making companies. I was privileged to have worked with John Piper himself as well as the other very talented model makers there, learning the primary importance of quality and attention to detail. I then spent some years at Stephen Greenfield Model Makers, working for photographers and magazine advertisers, on anything from full-size working props of a blast furnace bucket and a space capsule to a satellite for a themed swimming pool in Scotland!

For the National Army Museum in Chelsea, London, we created life-sized mannequins and landscapes to dress both a temporary gallery to celebrate the 12th anniversary of the Falklands War and a permanent gallery for the Burma Campaign in World War II. My favourite project was a model of a cross-section of a sailing ship, based on an original in the National Maritime Museum, to show how horses were transported in the age of sail. It was made entirely of apple wood for the National Museum of Racing in Saratoga, USA.

I have made prototype models of products and toys for Mattel's Barbie range. I have worked on over 40 films including *Charlie and the Chocolate Factory* and the James Bond, Harry Potter and Star Wars franchises. I have made all manner of models, including a spaceship for *Lost in Space*, a working submarine for *K19 The Widowmaker*, a collapsing house for *Sherlock Holmes A Game of Shadows*.

Children's favourites were *Thomas the Tank Engine*, the characters Max and Monty the dump truck twins, Colin the Crane, Madge the flat-bed lorry and Flora the steam tram.

Recently, when exhibiting Miniature Mansions products at doll's house fairs and explaining techniques to visitors, I realised it would be helpful to write out some technical guidance for enthusiasts to follow in their miniature creations.

INTRODUCTION

This book is not intended to be the definitive book on how to decorate a room in a doll's house. I will explain my own design process and the techniques I use to decorate a room using Miniature Mansions mouldings. Most of the techniques described can also be used for other mouldings using my step-by-step guide and templates. As well as describing the techniques, I also try to explain why I use them.

Throughout this book I explain technical terms and useful information, as well as specific techniques that you may need, in the shaded 'How to - Know How' sections of Chapter 6 The Knowledge.. I recommend that you read through the book before starting so you are familiar with the techniques.

I use spacers to locate the mouldings in position, therefore there is no need to mark their positions on the wall or ceiling.

This book has been written for all levels of experience. So please accept my apologies if at times it seems that I am teaching you to suck eggs!

I aim to show you in detail how to make a decorative ceiling. I chose a ceiling design to illustrate our techniques, as they are generally more complicated than walls. However, the same techniques are also used to make a wall design, and I will give you some pointers on wall designs towards the end of the book.

Where does one start when it comes to decorating a doll's house? Before I even consider putting any moulding into the room, I like to at least have an idea in my mind's eye of what I would like the finished room to look like from floor to ceiling.

As a starting point, I look through my reference books to give me inspiration for my design. I may not copy the design exactly but it will give me a guide as to how I would like the finished room to look. Other inspiration may come from:

- A particular style or period

- A particular piece of furniture you wish the room to display

- The little people who will inhabit the room

- A product (moulding) you would like to incorporate

- Reference books on the period you are interested in

- Pictures in a magazine.

My advice is to plan out what you want in the doll's house and try to imagine what the doll's house will look like when it is finished – this does not mean you cannot change your mind on décor later. Think through all the stages involved to see what steps need to be done before others. For example, lighting – will you use copper tape or hard wiring? Where will the light fitting go? Will the lighting in one room affect another (e.g. ceiling wiring for one room may go across the floor of the room above, so the flooring of that room cannot go down until the first room has had its ceiling lights installed)? It is simply a case of planning ahead.

Remember it's not that you cannot do it; it's about having the confidence to do it. Hopefully this book will give you that confidence.

I hope you enjoy designing and decorating your doll's house and creating beautiful rooms.

Always remember this is YOUR doll's house so you can do whatever you want!

Happy decorating.

Regards

John

CHAPTER 1

TOOLS

When it comes to tools I always buy the best I can afford - not to do so is a false economy.

ADHESIVE

To glue the mouldings into the doll's house you will need an all-purpose glue – UHU or Bostik is ideal. These adhesives retain a little flexibility even when dry, so should you need to move your doll's house (which may cause the doll's house to twist slightly out of shape) the mouldings will not move from their position.

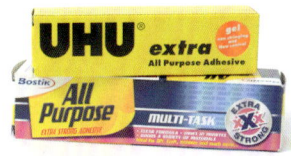

BENCH HOOK

This is a very handy tool and simple to make. As the name implies it simply hooks over the edge of the bench, allowing you to hold what is being cut firmly and stop the work surface from getting damaged. (How to Make and Use a Bench Hook – Know How 3)

BRISTOL BOARD

This is a smooth board. It is ideal for ceilings. Much easier to apply than a floppy sheet of paper, but thin enough not to be noticeable on the ceiling.

BRUSHES

Brushes are not really necessary, unless you are going to paint the inside of your moulding. If you want the best results, you simply must buy good quality brushes. I seriously recommend investing in Kolinsky sable. These are expensive, but worth every penny and if looked after properly they will last a lifetime. They are available from all good art shops.
(Brush Care –Know How 1)

CAR BODY FILLER

This is a polyester filler, which can be bought from any car accessory shop. It consists of a tin of filler paste and a tube of hardener, which are mixed together to use as per the instructions – as a general rule a golf ball-sized piece of filler needs a pea-sized amount of hardener.

Don't worry about getting the exact ratio of filler to hardener, as it is not critical (the manufacturers will probably tell you different). If too much hardener is added the filler will set quickly, if too little hardener is added it will take longer to set. Setting time should be approximately 20 minutes.

The filler can be mixed on an old piece of MDF, but a polythene surface is ideal because when the filler is set it will easily come off and the surface can be used again and again to mix filler.

But where do I get a polythene surface?

The lid of the car primer, plastic lids from large coffee tins or paint pots, or any large plastic surface. If you can't find one, you can use cardboard as a disposable mixing surface.

CUTTING MAT

These come in all sizes, and I think they are well worth the investment for two reasons. First, they save the work surface from cutting damage. Secondly they are self-healing, and don't retain the imprint of old cuts.

If a wooden board is used it will retain every cut, which can lead to the knife blade following one of the old cuts on the board and ruining what is being cut.

LIGHTER FLUID

Lighter fluid is a good all-round cleaner. Do not get it confused with lighter gas! It will remove marks and some adhesives, without leaving a stain. It is ideal for removing any adhesive left behind from adhesive labels. It is always best to do a test before using, to check that it will not have any adverse effects.

MITRE BLOCK

A mitre block is an aid, which guides a saw blade to cut a mitre (a 45-degree angle) on a piece of material allowing a corner to be made.

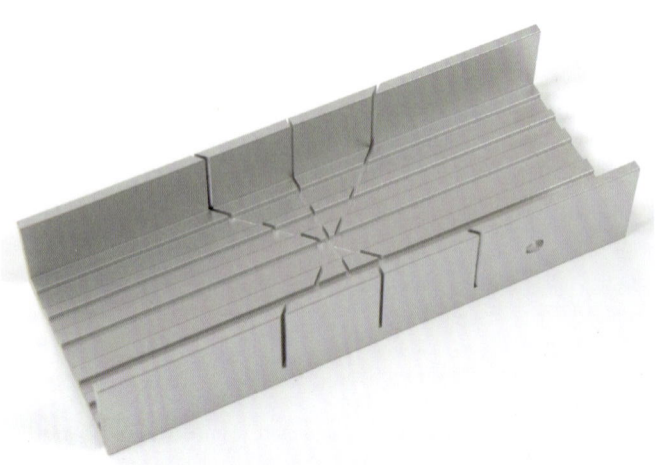

NEEDLE FILE

Needle files are small files, 6" long including the tang. Used by jewellers, model makers or anyone making small delicate items. They can be bought individually

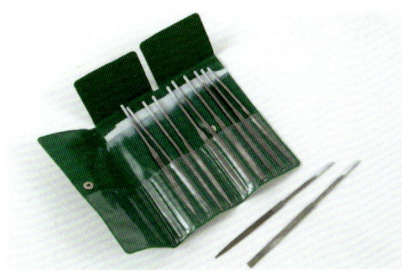

or in sets and come in different shapes – the most common are flat, round, half-round, square, triangle and knife. Are they a must-have? – Well, I could not work without mine.

PAPER

For drawing my designs, I always use a roll of lining wallpaper. You get a lot of paper for your money, so you can draw more than one design for a room and start again if you make a mistake that cannot be altered, all without worry over the cost of wasted paper. As lining paper comes on a roll, there is no need to join pieces of paper together and the length of the drawing is almost limitless, with a height of 22".

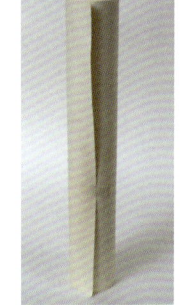

For designs with plain walls I paint the required colour on to copier paper then glue this to the walls with 3M Display Mount spray adhesive, although if the wall is larger than A3 then I use lining paper instead. All paper that is to be painted must be stretched first. The technique of how to stretch paper is described in chapter 3.

PENCILS

An HB leaded pencil is fine, but it must have a sharp point at all times. A good pencil sharpener is therefore essential

(I do not like using a knife to sharpen pencils as I find it is messy, wastes the pencil and it is hard to get a good point quickly) I also keep a piece of wet and dry paper handy (fine grade sand paper will do – about 600 grade) just to keep the tip of the pencil sharp, as follows. With the wet and dry paper on the bench, run the pencil lightly in one direction over it, twisting as you go, just to bring the point back between sharpenings.

What a palaver, why do I need a sharp pencil all the time?

The pencil needs to be sharp because as the point gets blunter, the line gets thicker. Then when you come to take measurements from the line, from what point on this thick line do you take them from? On a small scale this could make a big difference!

An alternative is to use a mechanical pencil with a 0. 5mm lead. When held upright it will always draw a line 0. 5mm wide.

PENS

I always go over my pencil drawings in pen. This is just something I do and it is not necessary, so I will not bore you with a long discussion on drafting pens!! However, if you do decide to ink in your design, buy a drafting pen with a point no bigger than 0.5mm.

RAZOR SAW

A razor saw is a small handsaw; the blade is very thin with small fine teeth and more teeth per inch of blade than a general wood working saw. This is an ideal saw for fine or delicate work. The saw will leave only the finest of saw marks, requiring little or no cleaning up afterwards.

RULERS

A steel ruler is another essential. Sorry, but any other type will not do! Always buy the best you can afford – you will need both a 12" and a 6" ruler. A 24" ruler is also useful, if your budget will allow.

SANDING BLOCK

This is simply a block with smooth flat edges that has sandpaper fixed to it with double-sided tape. It is used when sanding, particularly where it is important that the surface being sanded stays square or straight, and stops corners becoming rounded.

SCALPEL / CRAFT KNIFE

Knife choice is very much a matter of personal preference. I use Swann-Morton scalpel handles numbers 4 and 7 with a 10A blade.

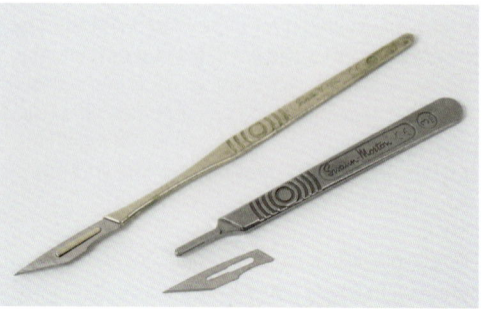

The heaver and thicker-bladed Stanley knife I can live without, as I find that it is too big and chunky and not suitable for delicate work.

SET SQUARES

For those who may not know what these are, these are triangles made (nowadays) in plastic. There are two types: both are right angle triangles but on one the longest side (the hypotenuse) is at 45 degrees and on the other it is at 60 degrees.

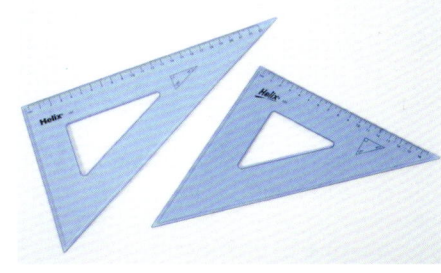

You will need a 45 degree set square. The 60 degree set square is handy, but not a must-have. They are available in sets along with a protractor and compass from WH Smith and other stationers, although the set squares in these sets are on the small side. I would advise that you instead just buy a bigger 45 degree set square on its own, available from the same places.

SQUARE

These are another must. The most useful are engineer's squares as they come in all sizes – the smaller sizes are perfect. I have all-metal squares from 2" up to 12".

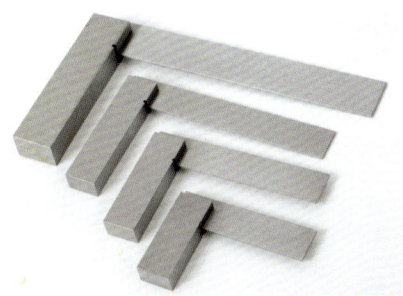

Woodworking squares are fine, but most are on the larger size, and I find the range of sizes of miniature woodworking squares limited. (How to Use a Square – Know How 2)

SUPERGLUE

This is a great adhesive for almost instant bonding, and ideal for gluing resin mouldings together. However, the bond is brittle, so it is not really suitable for use as a permanent fixing. Use it with the all-purpose adhesive to give a fast hold until the all-purpose adhesive has set, as this speeds up the process of fixing mouldings in place.

WHITE CAR PRIMER

A spray can of white car primer is required to prime the resin moulding. Two or three light coats are all that you need, then the mouldings can be painted in the paint of your choice. Should you require white moulding then the moulding will still need to be primed, as it will darken over time. White car primer can be purchased from any car accessory shop.

CHAPTER 2

MAKING TEMPLATES AND DRAWING THE DESIGN

In your mind's eye you have an idea of what you would like to achieve. Now it is time to get your ideas down on paper.

Why bother to draw out a design? To my mind this is the best way to avoid expensive mistakes, buying more mouldings than you need or, if you stop for any length of time, trying to remember what the design was!

At the drawing stage you can change your mind as often as you like – it only costs you paper and a little graphite. Any problems there may be will (hopefully) come to light at this stage, and better now than halfway through fixing the moulding in place.

Once you have a design that you are happy with it is possible to see exactly how many mouldings are required, to work out the cost and adjust the design if necessary to fit your budget.

Good news – you do not need the skills of a draftsman, only the skill needed to draw a straight line. The templates will deal with the tricky shapes and provide precision where needed.

The first stage is to make the moulding templates of the ceiling panels.

Making the templates

Step 1

At the back of this book are the outlines of all ceiling panels currently in our range. These outlines will help you design the ceiling and make the templates. The outlines can either be cut out of the book (they have been printed so they can be) or photocopied. If you use photocopies, please check the measurements against the originals as some copiers can distort the sizes.

Step 2

Now that you have your outlines *(PICTURE 2.1)*, they need to be glued on to cardboard. It can be glued as a complete sheet or cut out as individual items, then glued to card. It does not matter which you choose.

If you cut out individual items do not cut to the outline of the moulding but 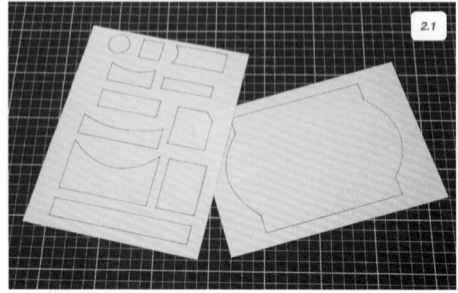 rather leave a bit of space around the edge *(PICTURE 2.2)*, then trim back to the outline once it has been glued to the cardboard. Any

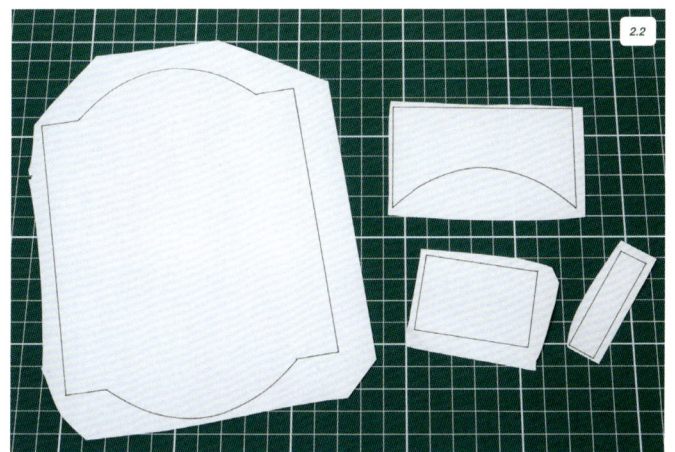

Overspray is caused by the force of the aerosol pushing some of the glue sideways, when it hits the surface that is to be glued. This overspray, although light, will spread some distance from the item being glued. Cover an area at least the size of two sheets of newspaper from the centre.

In the middle of this paper place an unopened newspaper. **(PICTURE 2.4)** Lay a sheet of outlines face down on to the top page of the newspaper and follow the instruction on the spray can to apply an even coat of adhesive on the back of the sheet.

card will do, even an old cereal box. I find that spray glue is easiest and quickest, but you could use watered down PVA glue as this glues paper and card as well as it does wood.

Spray adhesive

Some preparation is needed before the spray glue is used. The work surface will need to be completely covered with newspaper or any old paper **(PICTURE 2.3)** as there will be overspray, and keep the cardboard in a clean area away from the spraying.

Remove the sheet of outlines from the newspaper and carefully

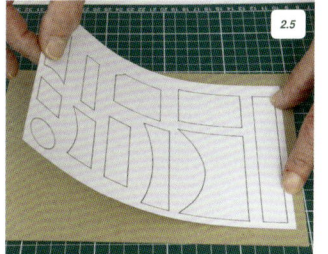

place it on to the cardboard by first placing the top of the sheet down on to the cardboard whilst keeping the other end in the air. Then, gradually working from the top, smooth the sheet down, all the time avoiding trapping air and creating air bubbles. **(PICTURE 2.5)**

If there is more than one sheet to be glued, open the newspaper so there is now a clean page that the next sheet of outlines can be placed on. Always turn to a clean sheet of newspaper for each sheet that is being glued to eliminate any chance of glue getting on to the front. Should spray glue end up where it is not wanted it can be removed using lighter fluid.

PVA

Less preparation is needed to use PVA glue, but it requires a 1" paint brush, watered down PVA and newspaper. With the newspaper this time opened at the centre pages – as with the spray glue a new page is needed for each sheet of outlines and in order to avoid getting PVA on the work surface it is better to work from the centre of the newspaper.

PVA as it comes out of the bottle it is too thick to be used with a brush on to paper so it needs to be watered down. The PVA needs to be of a consistency of between single and double cream (no need to be too precise!), but you need to be able to be apply it easily on to the paper.

To water down the PVA simply decant some of the glue into a small jar and add water a little at a time, mixing well until you have the right consistency. As I have said you do not need to be too precise – if you add too much water then add a little more glue. Adding water to PVA will not affect its adhesion, only lengthen the drying time.

Then it is a simple matter of applying the watered PVA to the back of the photocopies with a paintbrush. When applying the PVA, brush in only one direction, not backwards and forwards as this could result in the brush sticking to the paper and ending up with a crumpled mess! With the PVA applied, carefully place the outlines on to the cardboard making sure that no air is trapped to form air bubbles.

Step 3

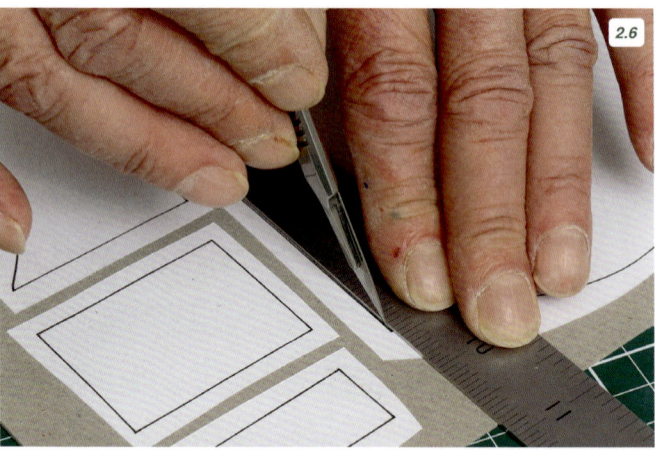

Once the glue has dried completely take a steel ruler and a scalpel or craft knife with a new blade and carefully cut out the shapes of the ceiling panels. *(PICTURE 2.6)* The reason that the outlines are backed with card is so when they are cut out they can easily be drawn around, using them as templates.

When cutting out the shapes always make sure that the steel ruler is covering the shape being cut, and then if the scalpel blade does wander off the line it will be away from what will be your template.

Make sure when cutting that the ruler is held down firmly and that the tips of your fingers are not over the edge of the ruler that is being used to cut along. Taking a slice of skin off your finger is very easy when cutting these out – double-check where your pinkies are before cutting! Once all the templates have been cut out you can move on to the designing your ceiling.

Ceiling design

A word about the scale of the drawing, I always do my drawing full size 1:1. This way it gives you the correct visual impression, and it leaves nothing in doubt.

Step 4

The first step is to measure the ceiling you wish to decorate. Then, taking the roll of lining paper, cut off a piece that is larger than the size of your ceiling plus an extra 2 or 3".

The extra space is for a legend i.e. notes. This is simply a space at the side of the drawing where information about the drawing can be noted.

So what information should be put in there? As this is only for you, use this space to make notes: the scale; which room it is for; which doll's house it's for if you have more than one project; whose and what are being used and where; the product code numbers; the name and page of the book being used as reference; what colours are to be used and where; paint manufacturer and anything else that helps. The more notes the better and these do not have to be written all at once.

Some of these examples could be written at the start, with others added as you go along.

Sadly, if you have to leave the project for any length of time, even if the drawing stage is finished, believe me you will find it hard to recall what you had intended to do. I know, I have done it myself! The notes will help you get back on track.

Step 5

Using masking tape on each corner, tape the paper on to a flat board. *(PICTURE 2.7)* Now you need to draw the outline of the ceiling on the paper. I do this by first drawing a base line with steel ruler and pencil about 20mm from the bottom of the paper, then, with the set square to the left or right of the paper, draw a line at 90 degrees to the base line, again about 20mm in from the edge of the paper. You should now have what looks the letter 'L'. *(PICTURE 2.8)*

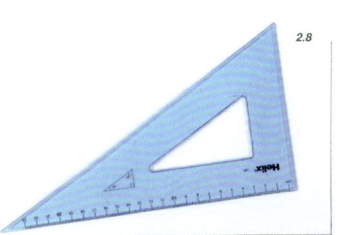

From these two lines you can measure and draw the last two lines to complete the outline of your ceiling. Once you have the complete outline of the ceiling, mark on the drawing which side is the front of the doll's house. *(PICTURE 2.9)*

The design being used to illustrate our techniques does not have a chimney breast, however if your rooms have them, these must be drawn on. (HOW TO DRAW A CHIMNEY BREAST – KNOW HOW 4)

Step 6

The first item that must be drawn on is the cornice (the moulding round the edge of the ceiling), because, as you will see, this makes the area that your design must fit into smaller than the overall ceiling size. There are many on the market for you to choose from and once you have chosen one you will need to know its depth. For the purposes of this book I have chosen SM71, the depth of which is $5/16$".

Draw the depth of the cornice moulding around three sides on the ceiling outline, including any

chimney breast. The fourth side will not have a cornice, as this is the front of the doll's house. *(PICTURE 2.10)* Where the mouldings meet in the corner, draw a line from the outside corner of the room to the inside corner (nearest the centre of the room) of the cornice, where the mouldings meet. *(PICTURE 2.11)* Chapter 3 will refer to this line, which shows the direction in which a mitre will need to be cut.

Mark on the outline the centre point of the room. I prefer my design to be equally spaced between the cornice and the front of the house, which means that the centre of the ceiling from back to front is now further forward than the actual centre of the room because there is a cornice on the back wall and not on the front. I find the centre by drawing two diagonal lines between the inner corners of the cornice, and not of the actual ceiling to the edge of the cornice at the front of the room, and marking where they cross as the centre. *(PICTURE 2.12)*

It is always best to double-check measurements, so measure the distance between the centre point to the cornice on one side, then check that it is the same measurement on the other side. Now check the measurements from the back to the front, by measuring first from the edge of the cornice to the centre mark, then from the front edge of the room to the centre mark. These measurements must be the same.

Now that I have marked the centre point, I like to draw a centre line from back to front and a centre line left to right effectively dividing the ceiling into quarters. This line is a useful point from which measurements can be taken. *(PICTURE 2.13)*

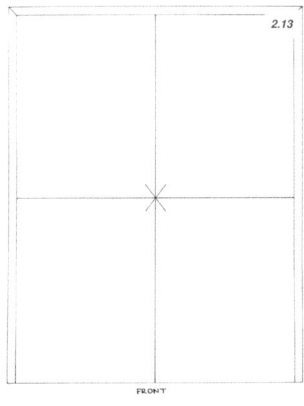

Step 7

With the outline now drawn and the centre lines in place, you can start the fun part of designing your ceiling. Taking the templates you cut out earlier, lay them on the ceiling outline. Move them around and try different combinations, until you a have a design you like. At this point the templates do not need to be accurately placed.

It well worth at this stage bearing in mind where the ceiling lights would fit into your design. You may find that you have more than one design that you like, in which case I suggest that you draw both designs so you can compare them side by side. If you have more than one design in mind it is well worth your while to scribble down a very rough outline of the designs on a piece of paper as a reminder, as after working on and finishing the first design you will have forgotten the others.

Step 8

Once the design (or designs) has been decided on it needs to be drawn out more accurately. There are several reasons why this is necessary:

1. Once drawn with all the mouldings in position you can then see whether the design is as good as you had thought.

2. Drawing the design this way proves that it will fit into the area of the ceiling.

3. The drawing will be used to measure and cut spacers that will make the fixing of the mouldings into your doll's house very easy, and does away with the need to measure or mark the ceiling.

4. Once the drawing is finished it is then possible to see the exact number of mouldings that will be needed, and you can accurately calculate the cost of the design.

5. You can see how mouldings made by different companies would work in combination.

This way of drawing out a design can be used for any mouldings, not only Miniature Mansions. As long as you know the dimensions of the mouldings then it is a simple matter of cutting the shape out in cardboard and using it as a template to incorporate into the design.

So now to make the accurate drawing. All this means is that the templates required for the design are marked out so they are equally spaced in relation to each other and as a group in relation to their placement on the ceiling itself, and so each template is drawn

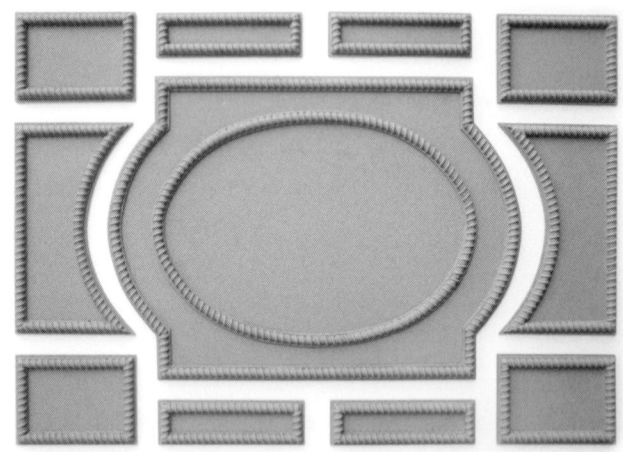

2.14

around in its correct position. To explain how I work out the position of each panel, I will use our ceiling panel set CPS 3 as an example. **(PICTURE 2.14)** The ceiling size I have chosen is 11½" x 14¼".

Step 9

If your design uses only one moulding see SINGLE MOULDING DESIGN – KNOW HOW 5 or if a group or pattern of moulding are repeated in a design see REPEATED GROUP OR PATTERN OF MOULDINGS IN A DESIGN – KNOW HOW 6.

On the ceiling outline, place the templates into roughly the position you would like the design to be on the ceiling. **(PICTURE 2.15)** Measure the distance between the cornice and the template on both sides of the design, making a note of the sizes. **(PICTURE 2.16)**

These measurements are unlikely to be the same as the templates have only been placed roughly in position. Add these two measurements together then divide by 2 to give you the spacing for each side of the design. Call this measurement 'A' and make a note of this on the outline as it will save you time later when making the spacers.

Measure the space between the inside edge of the cornice on the back wall and the template. Then measure the space between the front edge of the doll's house and the template. Again, these measurements are unlikely to be the same so again add these two measurements together and divide by 2 to give you the spacing for

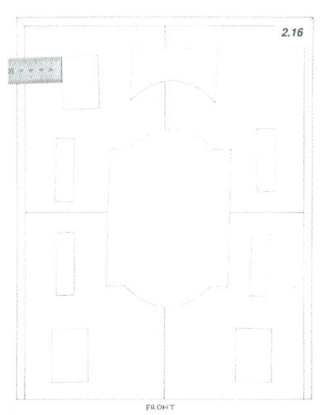

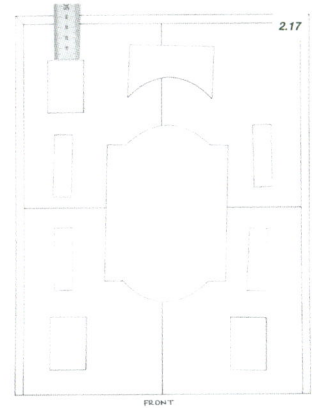

Step 10

Carefully place the corner template in place, making sure that the edges are in alignment with the perimeter lines. Hold the template down firmly and draw around it, ensuring it does not move in the process. *(PICTURE 2.19)* Repeat for each corner.

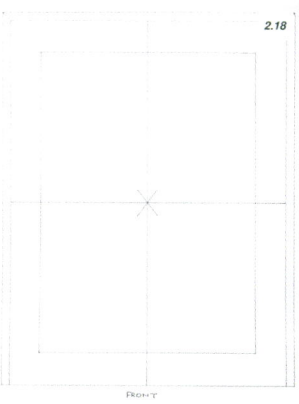

the front and back of the design. Call this measurement 'B' and make a note of this on the outline. *(PICTURE 2.17)*

Measurements A and B can be rounded up or down to the nearest millimetre or $\frac{1}{6}$ of an inch, depending on whether you are using imperial or metric; this just makes life easier.

On your drawing, draw a line down each side at a distance of A from the inside edge of, and parallel to, the side cornice. Then draw a line at the back, at a distance of B from the inside edge of, and parallel to, the back cornice, then finally again using measurement B draw a line parallel to the front, this time measuring from the front edge. *(PICTURE 2.18)* These are the perimeter lines, forming the outer edge of your ceiling design. Write A and B on the drawing in the appropriate spaces.

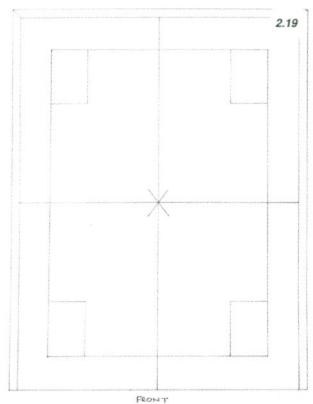

Step 11

Next you will need to mark the positions of the four side templates (two each side). As there are two templates, there are three spaces along this edge, one at each end of the mouldings and one in the middle. First put the two templates on the perimeter line adjacent to one of the corner mouldings and measure the space from the end of both templates to the inner edge of the opposite corner moulding. **(PICTURE 2.20)**

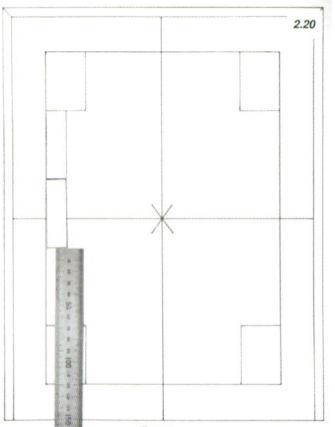

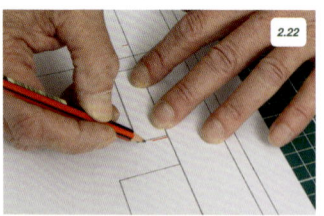

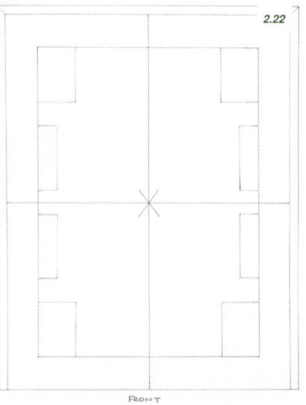

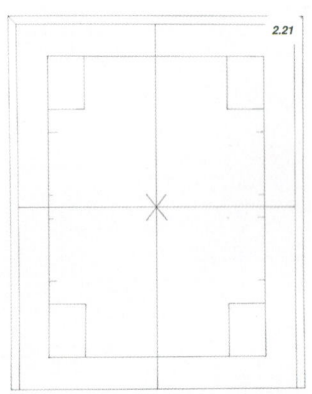

This time, the measurement must be divided by three. Call this measurement 'D', and mark on the outline. This dimension can NOT be rounded up or down. Measure distance D along the perimeter line from the edge of each corner moulding on each side. **(PICTURE 2.21)**

Place the two templates on these marks along the perimeter line, then check that the space in the middle is also equal to measurement D. If all spacings are correct, then mark around the templates taking care as before. **(PICTURE 2.22)**

If the space in the middle is not the same as the spaces at each end, then there are three possible reasons why:

1. The maths has gone wrong.

2. The lines on the drawing are too thick, making measurements inaccurate.

3. The design is such that it requires measurements to be down to or smaller than $1/64$ of an inch, or fractions of a millimetre.

If there is a big difference, the first thing to do is check 1 and 2 of above and correct where necessary. Should it be number 3, and the spacing is only off by a fraction. This is not something to be concerned about.

Do not get hung up on whether it should be this or that size. What is most important is that it looks right. Quite often in my work as a model maker I find that I have scaled things accurately but they look wrong, so I need an adjustment so it looks right. IF IT LOOKS RIGHT IT IS RIGHT!

Step 12

Now you will need to position the centre template between the two corner mouldings at the front and the back of the design. Place the template up to the edge of one of the corner mouldings you have already drawn around, and measure the distance from the end of this template to the inner edge of the opposite corner moulding. *(PICTURE 2.23)* Divide this measurement by 2, to determine the space on each side of the template between the two corner mouldings. Call this measurement 'C' and note on the outline – this measurement can NOT be rounded up or down.

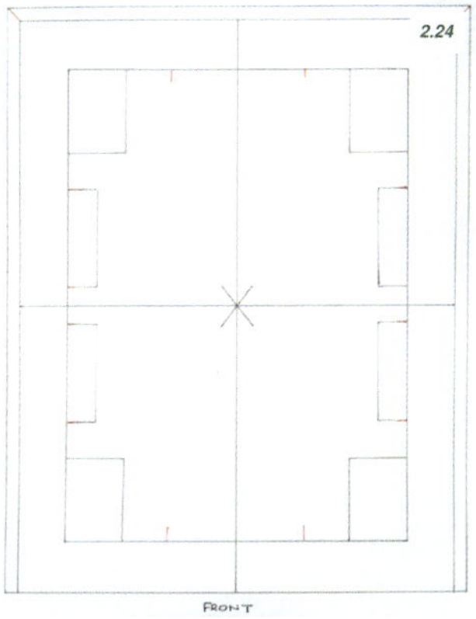

Measure the distance of measurement C from the edge of each corner moulding and mark it on the perimeter line *(PICTURE 2.24)*. Place the centre template on the perimeter

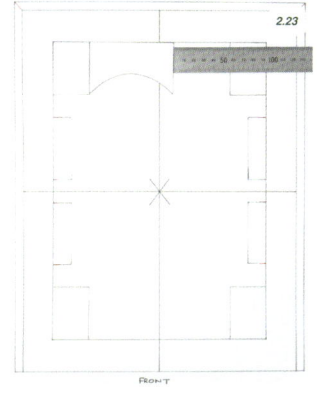

line between these two marks *(PICTURE 2.25)*, hold down firmly and carefully draw around the template. *(PICTURE 2.26)*

Step 13

Finally comes the placing of the centre panel.

On to the template draw horizontal and vertical centre lines. *(PICTURE 2.27)* Place this template on to the drawing and align the centre lines on the

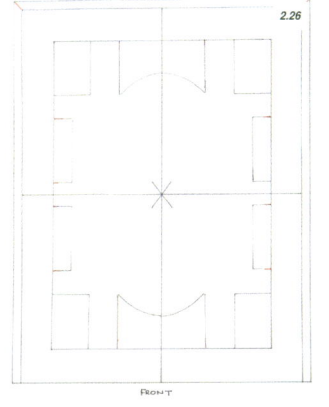

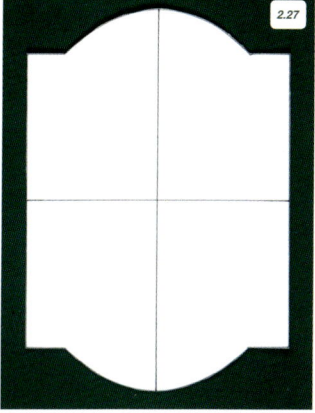

19

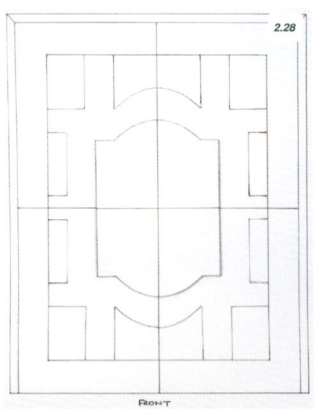
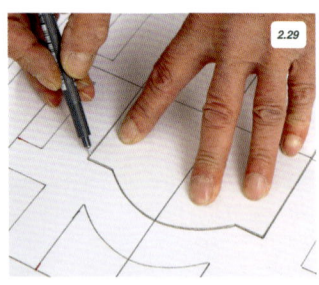

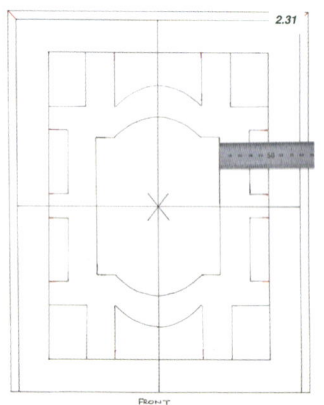
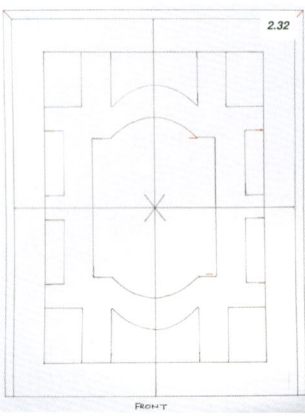

template with the centre lines on the drawing. *(PICTURE 2.28)* With the template in position, hold it down firmly and draw around it. *(PICTURE 2.29)* Now measure the distance from the corner of centre moulding outline to the edge of the moulding outline in the corner. *(PICTURE 2.30)* This will be measurement E. Now measure from the edge of the centre moulding outline to the edge of side mouldings outline. This will be measurement F. *(PICTURE 2.31)*

The drawing is now complete. *(PICTURE 2.32)* Now is the time to have a good look at the final design, as this is the exact positioning of the mouldings. Does it work? Do you like it? If there are any changes you would like to make – maybe the design looks cramped, or lost on the ceiling – now is the time to make those changes.

At this point, if you wish to make changes, you can either alter the drawing or redraw it completely. The only cost to you is your time, a piece of paper and some graphite. That's a lot better than fitting your design into your doll's house then wishing you had changed it. At that point any change may be costly and involve a lot more work and money, or you end up living with a room that you are not happy with.

Now that the drawing is finished and you are completely happy with the design, you can purchase the mouldings that are required. When the mouldings arrive, check them against the drawing to make sure they fit the outlines as drawn.

Chapter 3

PREPARATION OF THE ROOM AND THE MOULDINGS

It's now time to start getting everything ready for the final stage of decorating the ceiling.

At this stage you need to decide how and with what the walls will be decorated – that is if you have not already decorated them. If they are already decorated, that's fine. If the rooms are not already decorated, then there are two options, painting or wallpapering. You must also consider whether to decorate the walls of the room before or after the cornice is glued into place. If the cornice is glued in before the walls are decorated, then the painting or wallpapering will need to be very carefully done to fit perfectly up to the cornice.

I prefer to decorate the walls and ceiling before the cornice is fitted, as the cornice can then be glued on top of the paper or paint. This not only avoids the tricky process of aligning paper or painting up to the cornice, but also allows you to cut the wallpaper slightly smaller than the actual size of the room, which will make fitting easier. The cornice will cover any gap between paper and ceiling; a skirting board or wainscot will cover gaps between floor and paper.

Let's look at painting first.

What paint should you use? I recommend matt emulsion. It can be bought in small quantities from DIY stores in the form of match pots or samplers. I choose matt paint as it just looks right – gloss or semi-gloss looks wrong, to my eye. As I said earlier, some things just look right or wrong at sight.

Whilst on the subject of paint and what looks right or wrong, one tip from my days as an architectural model maker is never to use white paint on your doll's house as it will stand out like a sore thumb. If you want something to be white, then use an off-white. When I need white on any project I use white car primer.

White car primer is in fact off-white. Another tip is to spray white primer on to some white card (about 4" square), then take this card to a DIY store paint department as a sample where they will scan it and supply you with a sample of matt emulsion in the same colour as the white primer.

The primer I like to use and recommend is Hycote plastic primer, which should be available from small independent car accessory shops.

There are two ways that the paint can be used to cover the walls and ceiling.

Option 1: Apply the paint directly on to the wall and ceiling
Option 2: Apply the paint on to paper then glue the paper on to the wall or ceiling.

Step 14

Option 1: Apply paint directly

This would appear to be the simplest option, and of course it is. But if it is not done with care the finished paint surface will be disappointing. The answer to a good paint finish is the brushes used and the way the paint is applied.

First the brushes. In chapter 1, I recommended the use of Kolinsky sable brushes. However, painting a wall or ceiling requires a larger brush for which Kolinsky brushes are prohibitively expensive and a waste of money. The brush I use for painting large areas is a ¾" Daler-Rowney Sapphire range brush, available from art shops. These are not cheap but are well worth it.

A word of warning! As emulsion is water-based, any ironwork that has to be painted (hinges etc) will rust from the water in the paint unless they have been sealed and this will come through the paint finish. So before starting to paint, all metal surfaces must be painted with a white oil-based undercoat.

Apply the emulsion paint in even strokes, always brushing in one direction at a time whether from back to front or top to bottom, smoothing out any excess paint that may be left by the brush stroke. Do not be tempted to brush the paint in zig-zags, up and down, or any other motion. Painting the room will take more than one coat, especially where undercoat has been applied to protect metal items from rusting. Do not be tempted to try to cover the wall or ceiling in one go.

Once the paint is dry, apply the next coat in the opposite direction to the last coat. Repeat this process until there is a solid colour. This will produce a smooth paint surface.

If you choose this method to decorate the walls and ceiling, you can now move straight to step 17.

Option 2: Apply paint to paper first

This is my preferred method of decorating a room.

First, let's talk about what paper to use. For walls I usually use 80gsm copier paper. If the walls are larger than A3 then I use lining paper, although this does not give such a smooth finish. On the ceilings I use Bristol board, which is a thin, smooth cardboard, as I find the extra thickness helpful when applying to a ceiling. There is no reason for not using this board on the walls instead of paper, although I think it unnecessary and a little extravagant. However, before you can paint the paper and board it must be stretched. This often fills people with fear, but don't worry, it is a simple process. (HOW TO STRETCH PAPER – KNOW HOW 7)

Step 15

To paint the Bristol board it must be stretched first. Bristol board can be stretched in exactly the same way as paper, but the Bristol board will need more soaking, as it is thicker. Once dry, paint and cut off the board in the same way as for paper

Step 16

At this stage the walls and ceiling need to be decorated. Painting the walls and ceiling is explained in Step 14 – option 1. I reiterate the need to prime any metalwork and please bear in mind that if the ceiling is white it must be off-white.

You will need to apply the stretched and painted paper and Bristol board to the walls and ceiling. There should be three sheets of paper (two for the sides and one for the back wall) and one Bristol board for the ceiling, giving four sheets in all. As the papers and board were cut off the board with a steel ruler all the edges will be straight but they will probably not be square to each other.

The first step is to square one end on each of the four sheets, to one of the edges. You only need to square one end on each sheet. On the two sheets for the side walls, the squared end will go into the corner of the room and the other end will be trimmed back later. On the third sheet, which is for the back wall, the squared end will be used as a baseline to measure from. (HOW TO SQUARE THE END OF THE STRETCHED AND PAINTED PAPER – KNOW HOW 8)

Once all the paper has been squared at one end, it is time to trim the sheets to the correct height of the wall (leave the width for now).

Measure the height of the room, then cut all three sheets slightly smaller than this, by about $1/16$" or 1.5mm. Cutting the sheet smaller makes it easier to put the paper into the room, do not worry about any gaps as these will be covered by the cornice or skirting board.

The first sheet to go in is the sheet on the back wall. Measure the width of the back wall and cut the sheet a little longer than this measurement, by ½" or 12mm, as you want the ends of this sheet to go around the corners of the room and overlap with the side sheets. Once cut to size make a small mark on the bottom edge of the sheet to mark the centre. Mark the centre of the back wall and these marks will help to position the paper.

Cover the work surface in paper, as before, ready to spray the back of the sheet with adhesive. Spray the sheet following the instructions on the can. Now carefully place the sheet of paper into the room. First lean the sheet of paper so only the bottom edge of the paper is touching any surface. Align the bottom edge of the sheet with bottom edge of the room and the centre marks to each other. Once in position, slowly move the sheet upright. Once upright, apply slight pressure to the centre of the paper with your finger tip so the paper will stay in position.

With the paper now in position but not yet firmly glued, take a piece of kitchen roll. Working outwards from the centre to one side, smooth the paper from top to bottom until about 1" or 25mm from the corner.

Hold the end of the paper away from the side of the room so it cannot stick to it. It is very important when pressing the paper into the corner that the end of the paper does not stick to the side, as this will prevent the paper going into the corner and risks the paper tearing. Smooth the last 1" or 25mm down and into the corner and make a crisp corner, then smooth the remainder on to the side wall where it will overlap. Now repeat this process on the other half of the sheet.

Now that the back wall has been papered you can move to paper the sides of the room.

You have already trimmed the paper to the correct height, and now need to cut it to the length of each wall. Measure the side of the room then use this measurement to measure the paper from the squared end. Again, cut the paper about 1" or 25mm overlong, as excess will be trimmed later. Using the same techniques as for the back, paper the side wall. There is no need to mark a centre line as the squared edge goes into the corner of the room covering the overlap from the paper on the back wall. Now repeat this process on the remaining wall, leaving any excess paper at the front edge.

You now need to glue the Bristol board on to the ceiling. Cut the board narrower than the width of the room and longer than the length, as with the sides. Using the same techniques as before, position the squared edge of the board on the back edge of the room, then press the board into place working from back to front.

Once both sides and the ceiling are papered you can trim the excess paper and card at the front of the room with a scalpel, using the edge of the room as a guide. **(PICTURE 3.1)**

Once the room has been papered, cut out the spaces for the windows and doors. (HOW TO TRIM PAPER AROUND A WINDOW OR DOOR – KNOW HOW 9)

Step 17

For clarity I have not used a complete room with a floor, walls and ceiling, but show the ceiling only with upstands to represent the walls.

Now it is time to cut the cornice to fit the room. To do this you need to cut the mitres at the end of each cornice where they meet in the corners of the room.

The first part to be cut is the section that runs along the back wall. This piece has a mitre at each end. If you are not sure which direction to cut the mitre or how to cut a mitre see HOW TO CUT A MITRE – KNOW HOW 10 If there is a chimney breast in the room see HOW TO CUT A CORNICE AROUND A CHIMNEY BREAST – KNOW HOW 11

Cut a mitre on one end of the cornicing. Measure the width of the room, then measure from the tip of the mitre (the longest point) and mark this length on the cornice, on the edge that will be in contact with the ceiling. This mark will be the tip of the next mitre. Cut this mitre and now the mitres are cut on each end, **(PICTURE 3.2)** check that the cornice fits into the room. **(PICTURE 3.3)**

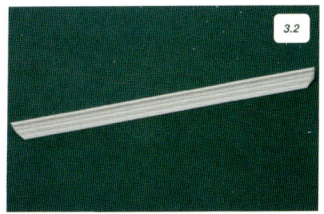

Step 18

It is now the simple matter of cutting the cornice for each side of the room. First cut the mitre on the end of a length of cornice. Then comes the tricky part, as it would at this point be useful to have three pairs of hands! Hold in place the cornice you have already fitted in place along the back wall. Then place the cornice you have just mitred so they abut each other in the back corner. *(PICTURE 3.4)* Check that they are a good fit – that there are no gaps and the two mouldings join nicely together.

While holding the mouldings in place, mark the side wall cornice where it exits the doll's house. Cut the cornice about ⅛" / 3mm longer then is required. (HOW TO MARK OUT AND CUT A CORNICE SQUARE – KNOW HOW 12) The extra length can be trimmed later.

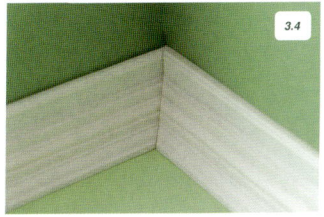

Repeat this process on the other wall. If there is a gap, then now is the time to fill it. (HOW TO CORRECT A POORLY-CUT MITRE JOINT – KNOW HOW 13) Put the cornice to one side until all the mouldings are ready for priming.

Step 19

Now it's time to work on the mouldings that will make up the ceiling design. Little work should be needed at this point, as they should have been checked for defects as soon as they arrived and the manufacturer informed, should there be any problem. At this point, check the moulding for mould lines and remove any with a scalpel or sanding block.

One moulding not included in this design is a ceiling rose. If the ceiling rose is a stand-alone feature it will only need a hole for the lighting cable. If it is to be combined with a ceiling panel, then this needs to be done now. This a simple matter of supergluing the ceiling rose to the appropriate ceiling panel.

Step 20

Next we turn to painting the mouldings. Resin mouldings only need to have two or three light coats of white car primer and they are ready to be painted. Plaster mouldings will possibly need more preparation and you should check the manufacturer's recommendation.

Although resin mouldings come in white as well as beige, if you wish to keep the white finish it is essential that the mouldings are sprayed in white primer as the colour of the resin will darken over time. For this design I require the mouldings to be white with a painted inside.

When spraying paint from an aerosol, the same steps need to be taken to protect the work surface as described in chapter 2 spraying adhesive. This is to avoid spraying the work surface and to protect the surrounding area from overspray.

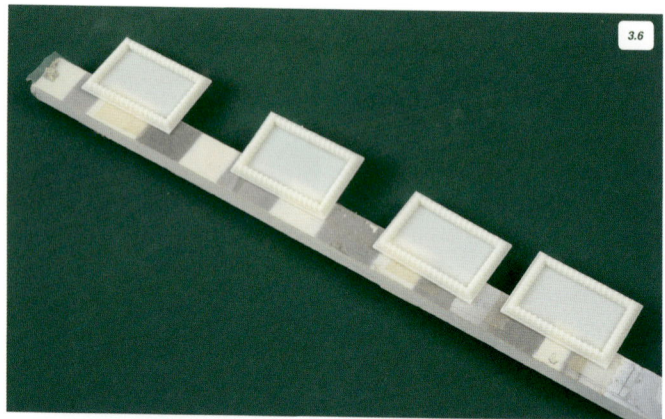

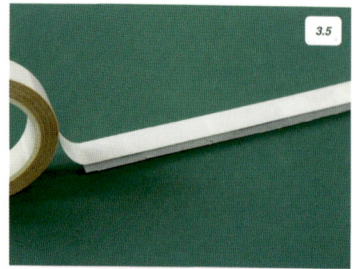

To spray the moulding I use an old strip of wood or MDF with double-sided tape down about ¾ of its length. *(PICTURE 3.5)* The double-sided tape is used to fix the moulding to the strip of wood. Only the edges of the moulding are placed on the tape to just be held in place, making them easy to remove once sprayed. *(PICTURE 3.6)*

Holding the mouldings over the covered work surface, first spray the outside edges. Position the moulding so this can be done with the spray can in a vertical position. *(PICTURE 3.7)* Next spray the inside edges. Finally spray the top.

The reason for only taping the moulding ¾ of the way down the strip of wood is so the piece of wood can be easily held by the last ¼ to avoid your hand being covered in paint. Always wear disposable gloves as some overspray will get on your hands.

The spraying is done one stick of mouldings at a time. Make sure that the mouldings on each stick are sprayed all over, then put to one side to allow to dry before the next coat. Once the mouldings have had their final coat of primer, put aside for the paint to dry and harden.

With the moulding taped to the wood it is possible to turn the moulding to make it easier to spray the sides. Once they have been sprayed the strip of wood can be placed on a work surface and the wood will stop the wet paint coming in contact with the surface.

Before spraying read SPRAYING – KNOW HOW 14.

Painting the mouldings. **(PICTURE 3.8)** Again my preference is to use emulsion paint, but you can use any type. (Decorative Painting – Know How 15)

Step 21

The spacers that will position the moulding now need to be cut out. A reasonably thick card is required, so the mouldings will not slip over the spacer when being glued in place. Refer to the drawing for the measurements written on your outline for the width of the spacers.

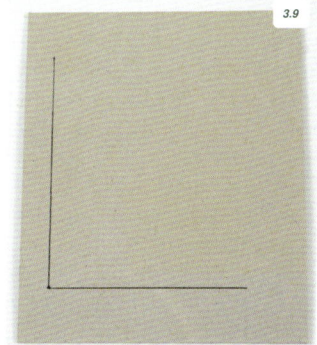

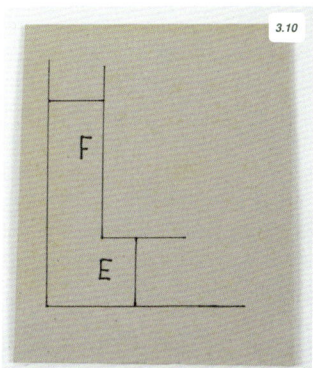

The first spacer you need is an L-shaped spacer to position the centre moulding. On the thick card mark a right angle using a set square. **(PICTURE 3.9)** One leg of this L-shape needs to be the width of measurement F and the other leg the width of measurement E. The length of each leg needs to be of sufficient length to position the moulding.

Once you have drawn the L-shape, check that each strip is the same dimension along its length, making sure the strips are not wider or narrower at the ends. If there is a discrepancy this must be rectified, even if it means drawing it again. It is important that all spacers have parallel sides.

Mark each leg with the appropriate letter F or E. **(PICTURE 3.10)** Now carefully cut out the spacer using a steel ruler and scalpel. **(PICTURE 3.11)**

Now cut four strips of card the same width as the measurements A and B: two strips for each. Cut one strip each for measurements C and D and mark each with its appropriate letter. Again, once all spacer strips have been drawn, check to see that they have parallel sides i.e. they are not wider or narrower at one end to the other. If not, then they must be adjusted or redrawn.

Measure each of these spacers to the same length, equal to the longest dimension of the room. They will be cut down later. Then carefully cut out all the spacers using steel ruler and scalpel.

Now all the spacers are cut out **(PICTURE 3.12)** it is time to start decorating the room.

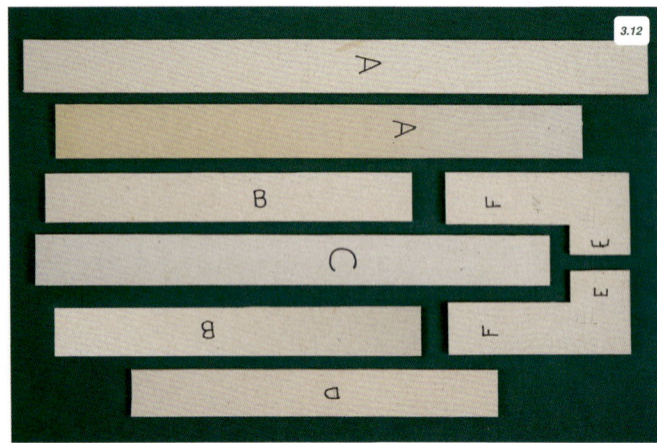

Chapter 4

DECORATING THE ROOM

Step 22

To glue the mouldings into place I use UHU or Bostik all-purpose adhesive as the main adhesive, with a small drop of superglue to hold things in place whilst this is setting. This way there is no waiting for the main glue to set, speeding up the whole process. Using superglue all over can result in a brittle bond, so I find the combination of both works best.

The first moulding to be fixed into the room is the cornice, starting with the piece along the back wall. *(PICTURE 4.1)* This piece goes in first because if the side wall cornices are in place it will be difficult to get the back wall piece into position.

Apply the all-purpose adhesive to the top and the back of the back wall moulding in four strips – two on the ceiling side, two on the wall side. Leave one space at each end and one in the middle, then dab a small spot of superglue in each space. Care needs to be taken not to apply too much adhesive, as when the moulding is pressed into place any excess glue will be pushed out. Now carefully put the moulding into place, making sure glue does not get on to the wall or ceiling where it is not wanted. Hold the moulding firmly in place until the superglue has set – about 30 seconds or so.

The two side cornices can now be put into place using the same technique. *(PICTURE 4.2)* When putting the side mouldings in place make sure the profiles of the mouldings are in line with each other, and that they are pushed right up to the moulding at the back making a good joint.

The ends of the side cornices will protrude out of the room as they were cut over-long; these can be very carefully trimmed back later when the glue has set using a razor saw, with the edge of the room as a guide. *(PICTURE 4.3)*

Step 23

The two corner mouldings nearest the back wall (mouldings 1 and 2) can now be glued in place (for moulding reference numbers see. **(PICTURE 4.4)** Gluing the mouldings into position will be made much easier if the doll's house can be placed on its back. If this is not possible, then the templates will need to be taped into place with de-tacked masking tape. (HOW TO DE-TACK MASKING TAPE KNOW HOW 16).

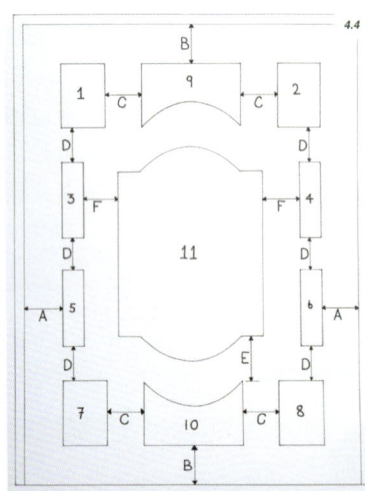

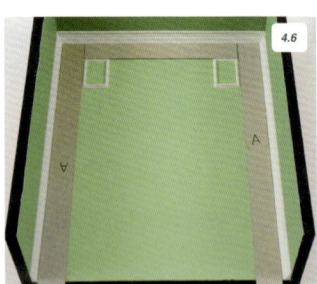

The first spacer to be put in place is B. This spacer will need to be cut down to fit using a scalpel and square. Fit this along the back wall and up against the cornice. Now put in place the two spacers A. These are placed along the side walls up against the cornice. Tape the spacers in place making sure the tape is not in the way of where the mouldings will be glued. Now the first mouldings 1 and 2 can be glued in place. Apply the all-purpose adhesive to the centre of the moulding, with a small spot of superglue. Then place the moulding into the corner formed by spacers A and B. Hold it there until the superglue holds the moulding in place. **(PICTURE 4.5)** Then repeat the process in the opposite corner. **(PICTURE 4.6)**

Step 24

The next mouldings to be put in place are the four side mouldings 3,4,5 and 6. Fit spacer D between the two spacers A and up against the two corner mouldings that have just been glued in and tape it in place. Mouldings 3 and 4 can now be glued in place. Apply glue in the same way as before and place the mouldings into the L-shape formed by spacers A and D. **(PICTURE 4.7)**

Step 25

Spacer D is now moved to the other side of mouldings 3 and 4 and taped in place. Then mouldings 5 and 6 can be glued in place. **(PICTURE 4.8)**

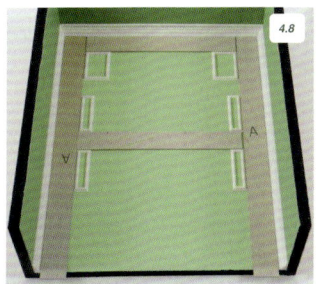 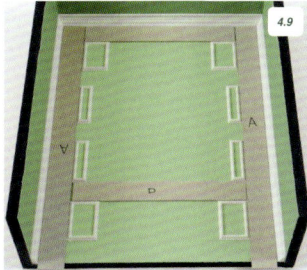 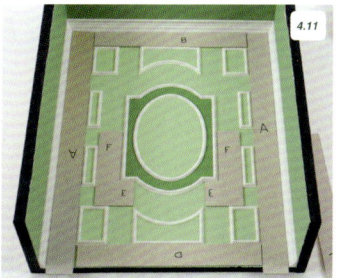

Step 26

Spacer D is again moved and taped to the other side of mouldings 5 and 6. Now the last two corner mouldings 7 and 8 can be glued in place. *(PICTURE 4.9)* Once this is done spacer D is no longer needed.

Now to position mouldings 9 and 10. To do this place spacer C parallel with spacer A. It does not matter on which side it is placed. Place the second spacer B up against mouldings 7 and 8. Then mouldings 9 and 10 can be glued in place at the top and bottom of the design. *(PICTURE 4.10)* When this done spacer C can be removed.

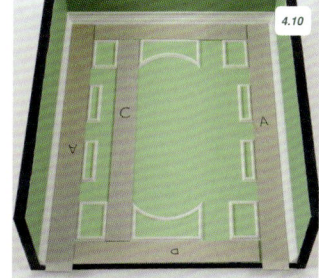

Step 27

The final moulding 11 can now be glued in place using the L shaped spacer E F. Place the spacer with leg F up against the side mouldings 5 and 6, with leg E against mouldings 7 and 8. This leg will need to be cut down to accommodate the shoulder of moulding 11. With the spacers in place check that moulding 11 will fit in-between the two spacers, to be ready for gluing. If the moulding will not fit between then trim the spacer down until it does, taking equal amounts off each spacer. If the fit is too loose then a larger spacer should be cut. Once satisfied with the fit glue moulding 11 in place. *(PICTURE 4.11)*

With this moulding in place all the spacers can be removed as the design is now finished. *(PICTURE 4.12)*

By way of illustration, I have included here a selection of pictures showing how templates were used in decorating the ceilings of our 'Chelsea' house.

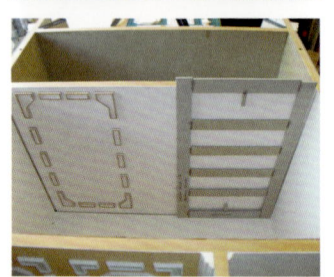

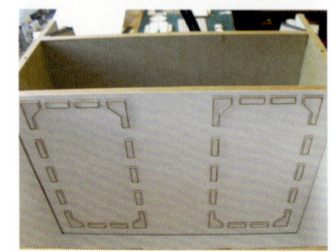

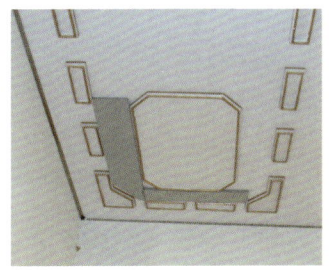
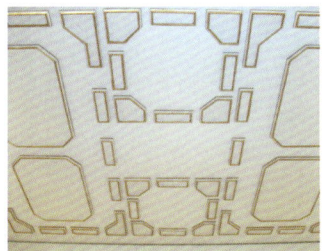

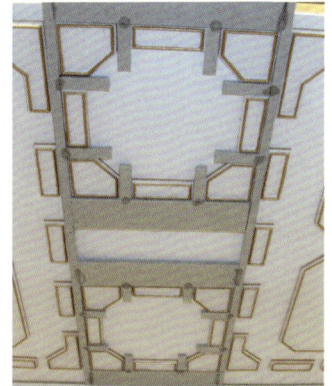
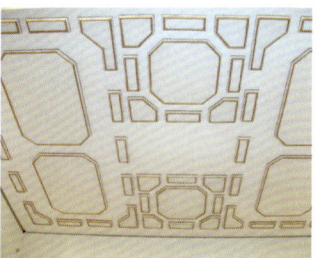

Chapter 5

WALL DESIGN

In the previous chapters I have examined in detail the techniques of how to design, draw and fix the ceiling mouldings in place. These same techniques are used when planning the design of the walls. I will only explain these techniques briefly here and give a fuller explanation of techniques specific to walls.

Design

This book contains template outlines of ceiling panels, which can be cut out. As most wall mouldings will probably be in the form of squares or rectangles there seemed little point in including templates of them. It is a simple matter to cut out squares or rectangles using either a set square or square. Some shapes can, however, be very ornate. At this stage, all that is needed for an ornate design is its basic shape – what is important is that it the correct height and width.

Having looked through the many doll's house websites and catalogues you should have a wide choice from which to choose the mouldings you wish to use to decorate the walls of your room. This may be a room with just a wainscot and cornice, a panelled room or a grand ballroom complete with pilasters and capitals. *(PICTURE 5.1)* Also at this point you will need to decide what is going on the ceiling. With the information gleaned from your

investigations you should now be able to produce the templates required. These can be made now or after you have drawn the walls of the room. (HOW TO MAKE YOUR OWN TEMPLATES – KNOW HOW 17)

Drawing

As with the ceiling design you need to draw out the area that is to be decorated. The only difference is that now there will be three drawings, one for each wall. This could be done on one long length of paper (if you have the space) or in three separate pieces. Measure the height and length of the room and draw this on your paper. Now you should have three oblongs, each representing one wall of the room. Mark on each drawing whether it is the left wall, right wall or back wall, and which way up it is.

There are two main areas where the wall plans will differ from the ceiling and one that they may have in common. The two main differences are:

1. There may be windows in the walls.

2. There is likely to be a door opening.

The chimney breast is common to both the ceiling and (one) wall. This detail should be also on the ceiling drawing. (Please note most Georgian rooms did not have chimney breasts, just an opening in the wall with an iron grate and a fireback).

The windows and doors need to be drawn on to the plan, as they may affect the design. If there is a chimney breast this should also be included. The detail of the chimney breast will be on the ceiling drawing and you can take its position and measurement from that drawing.

I will explain drawing these on to your plan.

But that's simple, I can do that without explanation!

I know you can, but I am going to explain it anyway – it pays to be cautious!

Marking out the window

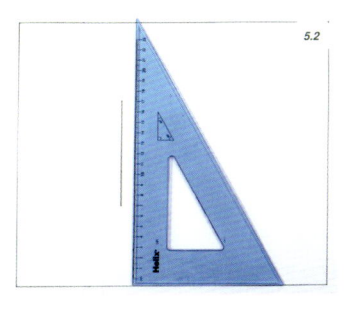

Measure from the front edge of the doll's house to the edge of the window. Then, measuring from the edge of the room drawn on the paper, mark this distance. Next, align the set square with this mark and the bottom edge of the drawing, then draw a line. **(PICTURE 5.2)** Then repeat this with a measurement taken from the back of the room to the back edge of the window. **(PICTURE 5.3)**

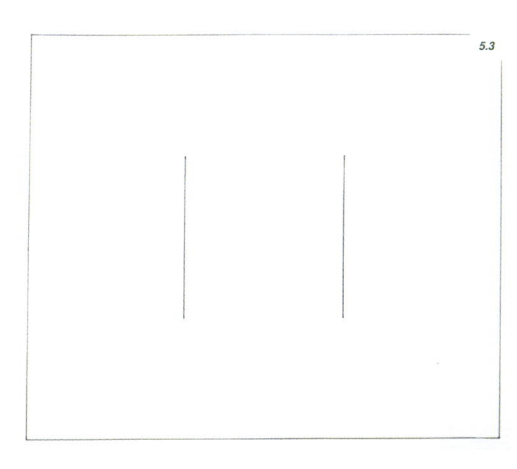

We now have to find the height of the window sill and the top of the window. If it is not possible to fit a ruler into the room, you can get a measurement by placing a strip of cardboard against the window from the floor to above the height of the window. Then mark the heights of the top and bottom of the window on this card.

Take this card over to the drawing and, aligning the card on the bottom edge of the drawing and along one of the lines already drawn, transfer the two marks on the card to the vertical line. *(PICTURE 5.4)* Repeat this on the other vertical line, then join up the marks to show the window outline. *(PICTURE 5.5)* As you can see from picture 5.5, I have marked the window with an 'X': this is so the window does not get confused with the moulding that will be drawn on later.

Mark out the door in the same way. The only difference is that there are only three lines to mark out i.e. the two edges and the top. *(PICTURE 5.6)* Again, I mark the door with an 'X', so the door does not get confused with the moulding that will be drawn on later.

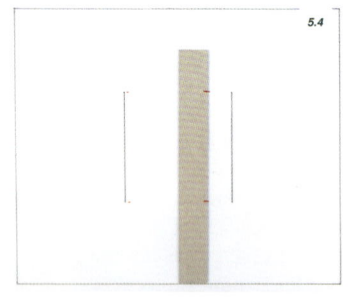

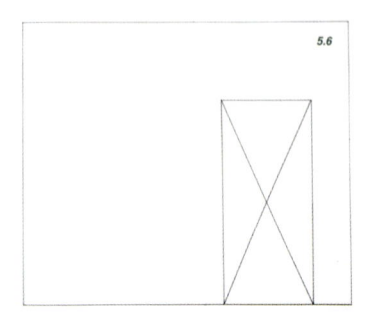

Next, mark out the chimney breast. This is simply two vertical lines drawn on in the correct position. A plan (i.e. bird's eye view) of the chimney breast should have been drawn on to the ceiling design. If you are not having a ceiling design in this room, then the chimney needs to be drawn now, as you may need this information to cut a skirting board or wainscot. (HOW TO DRAW A CHIMNEY BREAST – KNOW HOW 4)

Once any windows, door or chimney breast have been drawn on to the wall outline, you can begin the wall design. If you have already designed your ceiling then you can use what you have learnt from doing that to design the walls, referring back whenever you need to.

If you are only designing the walls then use this guide starting at chapter 2, Step 6 as the techniques are the same – just replace the word ceiling for wall.

The Knowledge

How To - Know How

Contents

1. BRUSH CARE — 38
2. HOW TO USE A SQUARE — 38
3. HOW TO MAKE AND USE A BENCH HOOK — 39
4. HOW TO DRAW A CHIMNEY BREAST — 40
5. SINGLE MOULDING DESIGN — 41
6. REPEATED GROUP OR PATTERN OF MOULDINGS IN A DESIGN — 42
7. HOW TO STRETCH PAPER — 45
8. HOW TO SQUARE THE END OF THE STRETCHED AND PAINTED PAPER — 47
9. HOW TO TRIM PAPER AROUND A WINDOW OR DOOR — 48
10. HOW TO CUT A MITRE — 48
11. HOW TO CUT A CORNICE AROUND A CHIMNEY BREAST — 49
12. HOW TO MARK OUT AND CUT A CORNICE SQUARE — 50
13. HOW TO CORRECT A POORLY-CUT MITRE JOINT — 52
14. SPRAYING — 55
15. DECORATIVE PAINTING — 56
16. HOW TO DE-TACK MASKING TAPE — 58
17. HOW TO MAKE YOUR OWN TEMPLATES — 58

1. BRUSH CARE

When you are ready to start painting and before you have put any paint on the brush, dip it in clean water (for water-based paint) or white spirit (for oil-based paint). Dry the brush and start painting. While painting, rinse the paint out of the brush frequently, even when using the same colour. Doing this stops paint building up and drying in the heel of the bristles, keeping the bristles supple.

Always clean the brush after use. It is important that there is no paint left in the bristles. When you have finished painting the best way to clean a brush is to rinse it in the cleaning medium (water or white spirit, depending on the type of paint) and keep changing the medium until no more paint comes out of the brush and the cleaning medium is clean. This may take 3 or 4 changes.

If you are using white spirit, do not throw the dirty white spirit away. Put it instead in its own container, as over time the paint pigment will settle in the bottom of this container and the now slightly discoloured spirit can be used as brush cleaner with only the last rinse needing clean spirit (saving you money not having to buy lots of white spirit!).

Never leave your brushes soaking in the paint or cleaning jar as this will bend the bristles.

After-care:

Sable brushes normally come with a little plastic tube over the bristles. This is to stop the bristles from getting damaged, so always put it back on when you have finished with the brush. If you are not going to use the brushes for some time after use, it's a good idea to put some Vaseline on the bristles. This replaces the natural oils that have been removed while painting. Leave them with the Vaseline on until you next use them, at which time clean it off with white spirit.

2. HOW TO USE A SQUARE

The correct way to use a square is all about how you hold it.

Place your thumb on the edge of the stock, holding the square against the edge of the material. Use your index finger to hold the blade of the square flat against the face of the material. Your remaining fingers should hold the material to stop it from moving. *(PICTURE 6.1)*

This way the square is held firmly in place up against the material but you can still move the square backwards and forwards by simply bending or straightening your thumb and index finger.

3. HOW TO MAKE AND USE A BENCH HOOK

A bench hook is a very simple (but very handy) tool / jig, which is easily made. Its purpose is to hold a workpiece steady while cutting and to protect the work surface (you may have seen me using one at doll's house fairs). It protects the work surface by preventing the final cutting stroke (when the saw goes through the piece being cut) from damaging the work surface, as instead the saw cuts the bench hook. This does damage the bench hook, but that does not matter as it is meant to be disposable. **(PICTURE 6.2)**

A bench hook works by simply hooking over the edge of the work surface, with the workpiece being firmly held against the stop at the top. **(PICTURE 6.3)**

A bench hook can be made from either plywood or MDF. All you need to make a bench hook is a piece of plywood or MDF for the base and two small strips of plywood or MDF to create the hook and stop sections. **(PICTURE 6.4)** The size of the base is a matter of personal choice. The length of the two strips need to be smaller than the width of the base by about ½". Once you have the pieces ready, simply glue one strip on the top of the base piece and one underneath, as shown in the illustrations. **(PICTURE 6.5)**

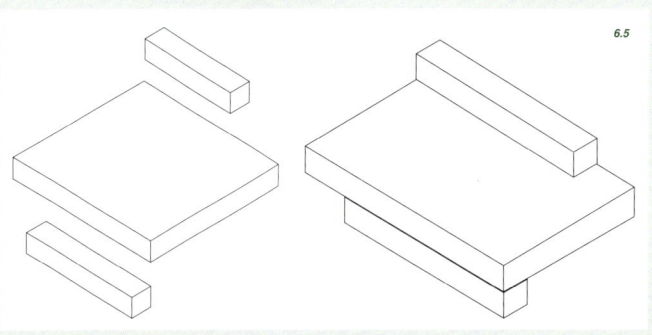

4. HOW TO DRAW A CHIMNEY BREAST

Drawing a chimney breast on the ceiling plan is very simple. A chimney breast can only be on the side or the back wall, not the front.

Lets' deal with a chimney breast on the side wall first. Measure from the front edge of the doll's house to the closest edge of the chimney breast, then mark this distance on the ceiling drawing. Using a set square, mark a line at right angles to the edge of this drawing at the mark that has just been made.

Then measure from the back wall to the edge of the chimney breast closest to the back wall, and mark this distance on to the drawing. Again, using a set square, mark a line at right angles to the edge of the drawing at the mark that has just been made.

Measure the width of the chimney breast; this measurement should be the same as the measurement between the two lines you have just drawn on the plan. If it is not, then you will need to check the first two measurements to see where the error has occurred. Then make the necessary adjustments, and double-check that the width of the chimney breast in the doll's house is the same as the distance between the two lines.

When you are happy this is correct, measure the depth of the chimney breast (distance from the wall to the front of chimney breast). Then mark this measurement on each line, measuring from the edge of the drawing (i.e. the wall). You can then join these marks up, which will complete the drawing of the chimney breast on the ceiling drawing. *(PICTURE 6.6)*

If the chimney breast is on the back wall, the measuring and marking procedure is the same as just described, only the measurements are taken from the side walls to the edges of the chimney breast.

If it is not possible to get a ruler into the room to make a measurement, then use a piece of cardboard. With a thin strip of cardboard (½" or 12mm wide approximately), put one end against the wall then mark on the cardboard the edge of the chimney breast. Then lay the cardboard on the drawing and transfer the mark to the drawing. Repeat as required.

5. SINGLE MOULDING DESIGN

If your design only requires one moulding in the centre of a room, then all that you need on the drawing are the cornice and centre lines, as at the end of step 6. **(PICTURE 6.7)** Mark the centre lines on the template along its width and depth, making a cross. Now, line up the template centre lines carefully with the centre lines on the drawing, and then draw around the template. The reason for the drawing, even when only one panel is being used, is so a spacer can be cut to aid the gluing the moulding in place.

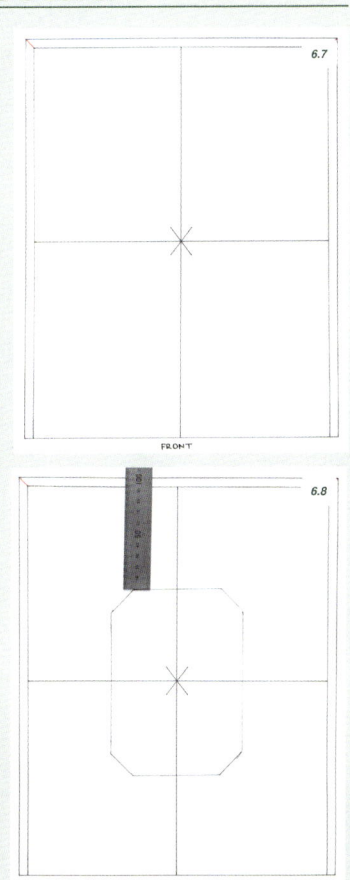

For this single moulding design all that is needed is one L-shaped spacer, which is placed in one corner of the ceiling up against the cornice at the back and one at the side, then the moulding can be glued in place up against the spacer. The measurement for the width of the legs is taken from the drawing. One leg should be the measurement from the edge of the cornice on the back wall to the edge of the moulding. **(PICTURE 6.8)** The measurement for the other leg is taken from the edge of the cornice on the side wall to the edge of the moulding. **(PICTURE 6.9)** The legs of the spacer should be more than half of the length of the moulding. **(PICTURE 6.10)** This is to ensure that the moulding will be placed squarely on the ceiling. (See how L shaped spacers are used in Step 27.)

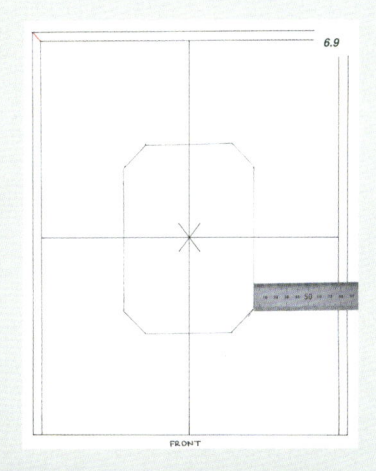

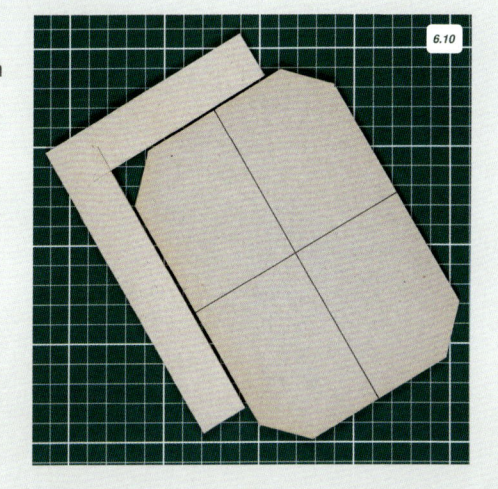

6. REPEATED GROUP OR PATTERN OF MOULDINGS IN A DESIGN

On larger ceiling designs, you may find a group or pattern of mouldings. Rather than having to draw this pattern more than once, draw only one pattern and then you can use copies of this to cut out and glue in place.

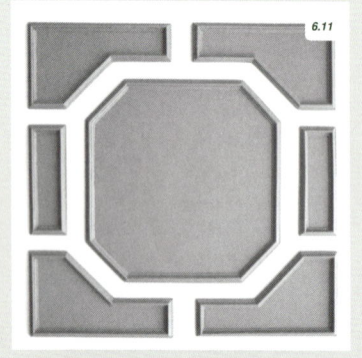

As an example, I have created a design that has within it four sets of CPS8 *(PICTURE 6.11)* with one SM106 in the centre as a boss for a chandelier, *(PICTURE 6.12)* and the cornice SM5. *(PICTURE 6.13)* This design has a round boss in the centre, with the other mouldings spaced out around it.

Step A

Take the drawing to the end of step 6 in chapter 2. The centre of the room has been marked out and the ceiling divided into quarters.

On the centre point of the ceiling draw the boss using a pencil and compass. To do this you need to know the radius of the boss. The radius is half the diameter. In this case the diameter is $7/8$", divide $7/8$" by 2 = $7/16$". Set the compass to this measurement *(PICTURE 6.14)* and draw the boss.

Step B

In one quarter of the drawing, place the templates into roughly the required position. CPS 8 is a square design, so once they are laid out, measure the group of templates from side to side and back to front. *(PICTURE 6.15)* As they were only placed roughly, the measurements will not produce an exact square, and you will need to equal them out to form a square. For example, if the measurements are 6½" x 7½", add 6½" and 7½" to equal 14", then divide by 2 to get 7" – therefore a 7" square is required.

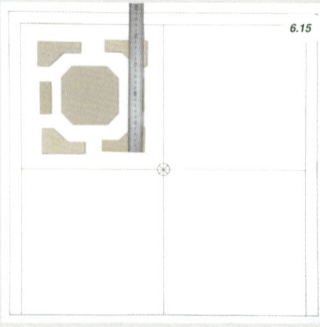

Draw and cut out the size of square you need and place it in one quarter of the drawing to check that you are happy that the square does not look too big or too small. If you are not happy with it, cut out a larger or smaller square until you are satisfied with the size.

Step C

Once you are happy with the size of the paper square, carefully place a corner template in one corner of this square then draw around the template. Repeat this in each corner. *(PICTURE 6.16)*

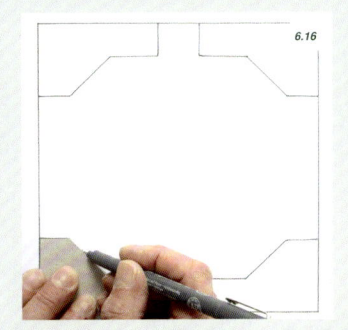

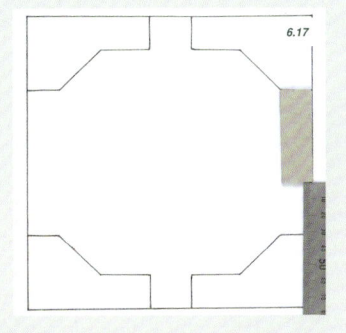

Step D

You now need to position the two straight spacing panels. Place the template up to the outline that has already been drawn in the corner, and measure the space from the end of this template to the edge of the next outline. *(PICTURE 6.17)* As the spacing needs to be equal, divide this measurement in two and call the measurement 'X'. Mark measurement X on the paper square. *(PICTURE 6.18)* You can now place the templates between the marks and accurately draw around them. *(PICTURE 6.19)*

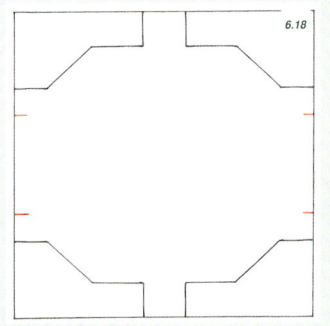

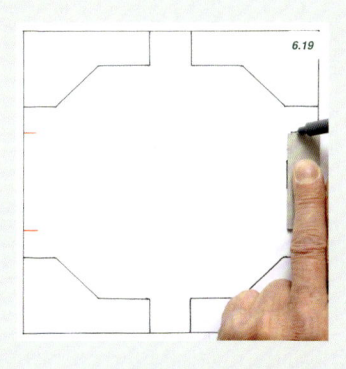

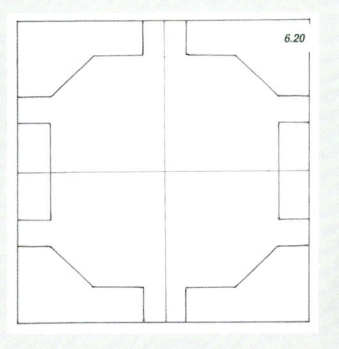

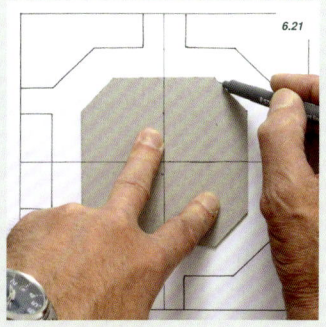

Step E

Placing of the centre panel. On to the repeat design and template draw a vertical and horizontal centre line. *(PICTURE 6.20)* Now line up the centre lines on the template with the centre lines on the repeat design and carefully draw around. *(PICTURE 6.21)*

Step F

The repeat design is now complete. *(PICTURE 6.22)* Now we need to make as many photocopies of this design as is required for the overall design. Check all the copies to make sure that the copier has not distorted them. These copies can now be cut out and glued onto the main drawing.

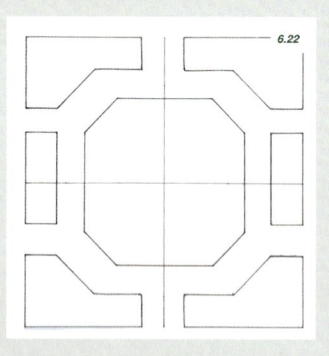

To ensure their correct position, each quarter of the ceiling plan must now have a vertical and horizontal centre line drawn on. Measure from the edge of the cornice to the centre line of the drawing, divide this measurement in two. Measuring this distance from the edge of the cornice make a mark at the top and bottom of the drawing. *(PICTURE 6.23)* Now join up these marks. *(PICTURE 6.24)* Measure from the bottom of the drawing to the centre line and again divide this measurement by two. Measuring this distance from the bottom of the drawing, make a mark on each of the two new centre lines that have just been drawn. Measure the same distance from the edge of the cornice at the back of the drawing and make a mark on each of the new centre lines. *(PICTURE 6.25)* Now join these marks. *(PICTURE 6.26)*

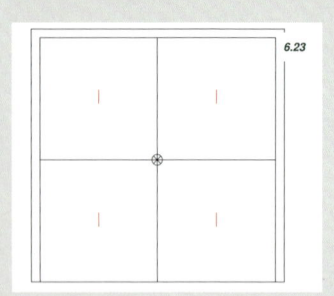

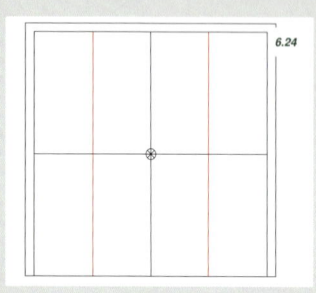

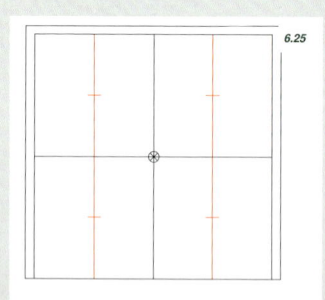

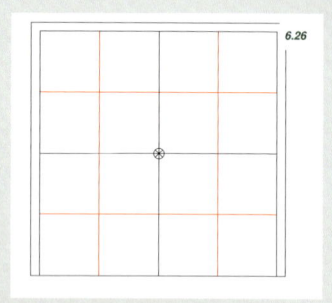

Each quarter of the drawing now has centre lines. The repeat designs can now be glued in place, by carefully lining up the centre lines in each quarter of the drawing with the centre line on a repeat design. *(PICTURE 6.27)*

7. HOW TO STRETCH PAPER

The reason the paper has to be stretched is that if it's not, it will wrinkle up when painted and will be useless. All that you need to stretch paper is a bowl of water, a roll of gummed paper tape (gummed paper tape called Gum Strip is available from art shops and comes in 2"-wide rolls) and a piece of MDF or similar.

The one thing to remember is that the paper needs to be about 1" bigger than the wall it is to cover. There are two reasons for this: (1) so the paper can be trimmed down to room size without having to worry about running out of painted area, and (2) because the paper will be gummed down to the board around all its edges and the gummed portion discarded. The board needs to be bigger than the paper by about 2" all round so that the paper can be gummed down.

Step A

Cut the three pieces of paper required for the walls, remembering to make them about 1" bigger allround than the size of the walls. A sheet of A3 copier paper should be larger than most doll's house walls. Cut a sheet of Bristol board for the ceiling (this will also need to be stretched if being painted, see step 15), again 1" bigger all round. Put these aside for the moment.

Step B

Cut two overlength (2" extra) strips of gummed paper for each sheet of paper to be stretched, one for the width and one for the height. Gummed paper tape comes on a 2-" wide roll, which is wider than needed. Fold each strip in half along its length, then with a steel ruler and scalpel cut the strips in half lengthways using the fold as a guide. *(PICTURE 6.28)* You should now have sufficient strips for all sides of each piece of paper to be stretched.

Step C

Collect everything together so that all you need is close at hand. You will need a bowl of water, the paper (and Bristol board, if being stretched), the gummed tape strips, MDF board and some kitchen roll. Submerge the paper in the water until soaked. You can tell when the paper is soaked as its appearance changes and it loses its stiffness. If the paper is too large for the bowl, move the paper around until all the paper is soaked. *(PICTURE 6.29)*

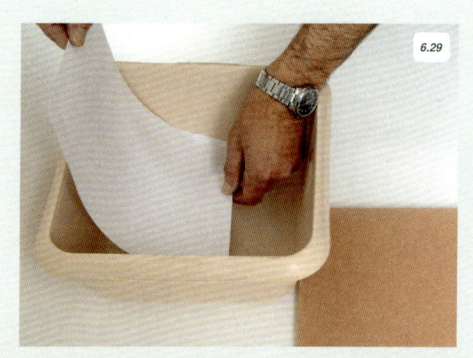

Take the paper out of the water and lay it on the MDF board. Do not worry if the paper is not flat on the board, as long as there are no creases. Run a strip of gummed paper tape through the bowl of water

(PICTURE 6.30) then use this to stick one edge of the paper to the board – with about ⅓ of the tape on the paper and ⅔ on the board. *(PICTURE 6.31)* Repeat until all the edges have been glued down with the gummed paper tape. Dab off any surplus water with kitchen roll. Now leave the paper to dry.

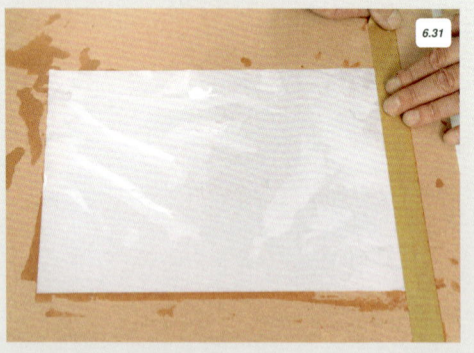

DO NOT try to flatten the paper – it may look lumpy and bumpy now but when the paper is dry it will be flat. Promise. *(PICTURE 6.32)* If you have space on the board to stretch more than one piece of paper at a time, do so. Once the paper is taped down leave it to dry.

Once the paper is stretched and dry, the paint can be applied. Leave the paper taped to the board to be painted, as it will crinkle when the paint is applied, then flatten when the paint dries. Apply the emulsion paint in even strokes, always brushing in one direction at a time whether from back to front or top to bottom, smoothing out any excess paint that may be left by the brush stroke. Do not be tempted to brush the paint in zig-zags, up and down, or any other motion. Painting the paper will take more than one coat. Do not be tempted to try to cover the paper in one go.

Once the paint is dry, apply the next coat in the opposite direction to the last coat. Repeat this process until there is a solid colour. This will produce a smooth paint surface. The paper will go lumpy and bumpy while being painted but it will flatten out when dry.

Once the painted paper is completely dry, cut it off the board. Place a steel ruler along the edge of the tape holding the paper to the board and cut the edge free using a scalpel. Repeat this for each edge. Repeat the whole process until there are enough sheets of stretched and painted paper to decorate the room.

8. HOW TO SQUARE THE END OF THE STRETCHED AND PAINTED PAPER

There are two ways that the paper can be cut square.

My preferred way is to trim the end of the sheet using a square. Place the sheet of paper on a cutting mat (I have cut the paper on a board for clarity) with its edge parallel to the bottom edge of the mat. Place the square stock-up against the edge of the cutting mat and paper (AS DESCRIBED IN KNOW HOW 2), with the blade of the square along the line you wish to cut. Now cut the paper along the blade of the square with a scalpel. **(PICTURE 6.33)**

If the blade of the square will not cover the whole of the paper, then place a steel ruler up against the blade of the square and trim the paper using the edge of the steel ruler. **(PICTURE 6.34)**

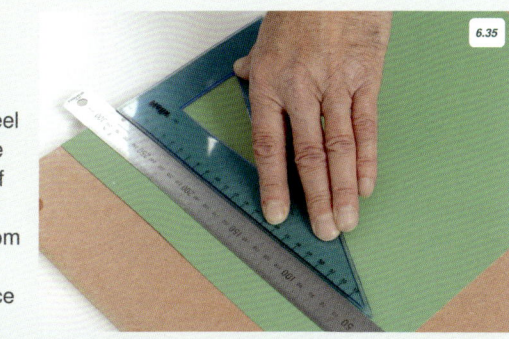

If you do not have a square then use a set square and steel ruler. Place the bottom edge of the set square along the bottom edge of the paper and place the steel ruler up against the other side of the set square. Trim the paper using the edge of the steel ruler. **(PICTURE 6.35)** When the paper has been squared, mark on the back which edges are square to each other. **(PICTURE 6.36)**

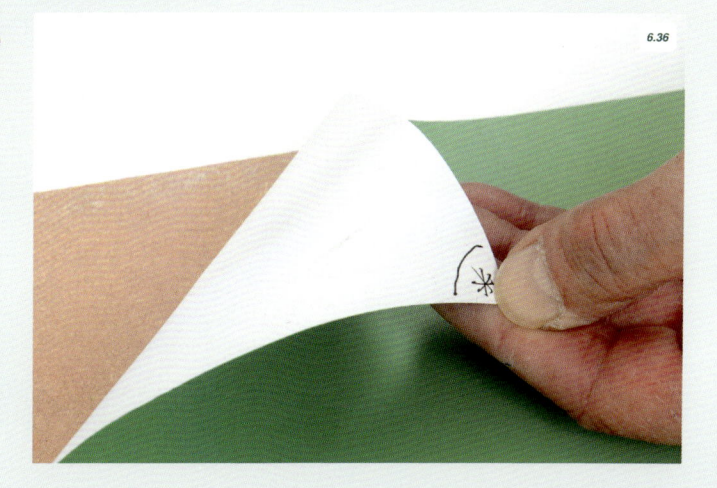

47

9. HOW TO TRIM PAPER AROUND A WINDOW OR DOOR

Using the methods I have described means that window and door openings have been papered over, so now the paper needs to be trimmed back. With a scalpel roughly cut out the paper covering the window or door. This will allow you to see what you are doing. Now the paper can be trimmed back cleanly and precisely around the opening, using a scalpel to carefully follow around the opening. **(PICTURE 6.37)** If you try to trim the paper while the window or doors are completely covered with the paper you risk damaging the window or door if it is in place.

10. HOW TO CUT A MITRE

A mitre is simply a 45 degree cut on the ends of two pieces of any material so when the two ends are put together they form a right angle – in almost all cases this is how the corners in doll's houses are made. So in less technical terms, we are making a corner.

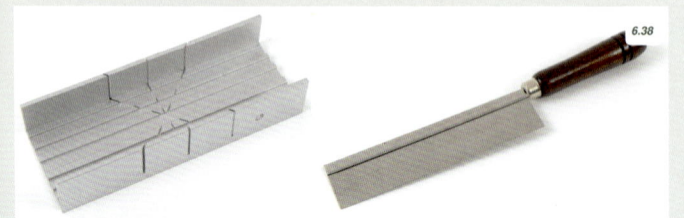

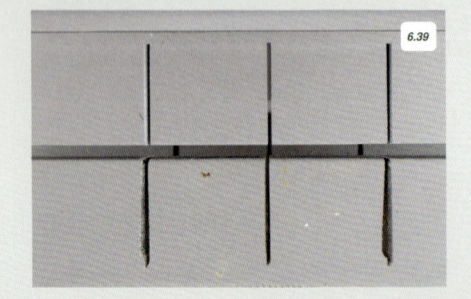

To do this requires a mitre block and a razor saw. **(PICTURE 6.38)** There are two main points to note: first, the razor saw needs to be sharp, otherwise too much effort is needed to cut a mitre on the moulding. The saw should do the work, as too much pressure on the saw will cause the blade to wander and not cut straight. This may also cause damage to the mitre block at the same time, which brings me nicely to my second point: before using the mitre block check that the slot used to cut mitres is not damaged. See how the slots in the mitre block at the top of **(PICTURE 6.39)** are straight, while the slots in the block at the bottom of the picture have been worn away by the razor saw. This damage will make it almost impossible to cut a good mitre.

Mark the moulding where you wish to cut the mitre and align this mark with the slot in the mitre block. Then, holding the moulding firmly in the mitre block, make the cut. **(PICTURE 6.40)** The secret to a good mitre cut is not to rush – let the saw do the work.

The most common mistake when cutting a mitre is cutting it in the wrong direction. The way to avoid this is to simply place the moulding on the drawing and mark the direction of the cut.

If you do not have a drawing, place the moulding up to its position in the doll's house and mark the direction of the mitre onto the moulding. This mark only needs to be roughly drawn, as long as it clearly shows the direction of the cut required.

11. HOW TO CUT A CORNICE AROUND A CHIMNEY BREAST

The chimney breast should be marked on your plan of the ceiling, with the width of the cornice drawn around it. You can mark the mitres on the drawing by simply drawing a line from corner to corner. **(PICTURE 6.41)**

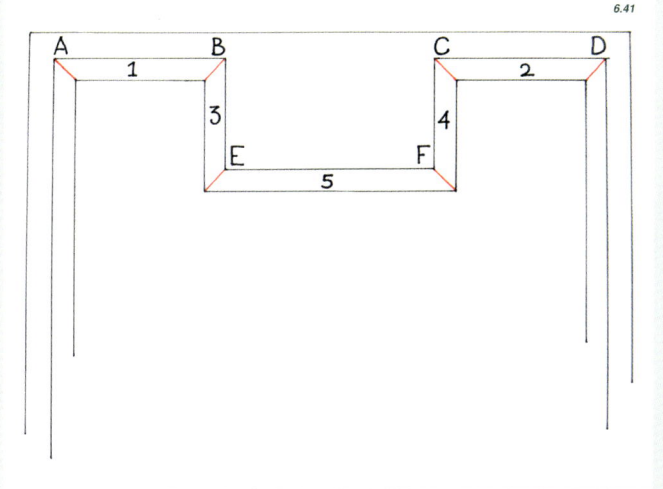

The first lengths of cornice to be cut are lengths 1 and 2. Taking a length of cornice, place it on the drawing in position 1 and mark the direction of the cut on the cornice for corner A. Then, using a mitre block and razor saw, cut the mitre.

Then take a measurement from point A to point B, measuring from the tip of the mitre that has just been cut, and mark this measurement on the cornice. This mark is the tip of the next mitre. Place the cornice back on the drawing and mark the direction of the cut. Then cut the mitre. This process is repeated to cut cornice number 2, taking a measurement for this piece from points C to D.

(There is no need to keep going back to the drawing to mark the direction of the cut, but I find doing this avoids cutting a mitre in the wrong direction. This mark does not have to be accurate in any way, as long as it is clear in which direction the cut needs to be.)

Mark and cut the rest of the cornicing in the same way as just described. With cornices 3 and 4 the first mitres to be cut are for points B and C respectively. For cornice 3, the measurement should be taken from points B and E and for cornice 4 the measurement should be taken from points C and F. Finally cornice 5 is cut using the measurement from points E to F.

12. HOW TO MARK OUT AND CUT A CORNICE SQUARE

To cut a cornice square (or anything else for that matter), the marking out is just as important as the actual cutting. This is where the engineer's square is essential. To make a square cut, you need to mark a line at a minimum on two sides of the item being cut, ideally on all four sides. The reason for this is that if the lines are not drawn accurately, the last line to be drawn will not meet the first line, so straightaway you can see that something is wrong, even before you start cutting.

For clarity, I have demonstrated marking-out on a piece of wood. Mark on the item where it needs to be cut. Taking the square (SEE KNOW HOW 2), hold the stock firmly against the item with the blade on the mark you have just made, then draw a line in any direction.

Turn the item so you can draw a line on the adjoining edge. Repeat the marking process, this time with the blade of the square aligned with the line you have just drawn. Repeat this on all four edges. **(PICTURE 6.42)**

Always work from the line that was last drawn. The last line drawn must exactly meet the first line drawn. If it does not, then the marking-out is not square and must be done again, as a square cut cannot be made. **(PICTURE 6.43)** This error may be because:

- The stock of the square was not held firmly against the workpiece

- Something is between the stock and the workpiece e.g. a bit of sawdust

- There was inaccuracy in the starting of one line from the end of the previous one

- The square itself is not square.

6.43

There is a simple way to check to see if a square is actually square. Using a piece of MDF or wood that has a straight edge, draw a line using the square up against the straight edge. Then flip the square over (back to front) and place the blade of the square up against the line that has just been drawn. The blade should be parallel to this line and match up with it exactly. If it is not, then the square is not accurate and needs to be replaced. **(PICTURE 6.44)**

6.44

Once you have drawn a square line around the item then it is ready to be cut. All that is needed is a sharp saw.

Why a sharp saw? It's not just to make your life easier, although it will. A blunt saw means that more pressure will be needed to cut, which makes the saw less controllable. Using too much pressure on a thin-bladed saw can cause the blade to distort and wander off the line.

Let the saw do the work. This simply means take your time and don't force the saw; use only enough pressure so that the saw cuts. If too much pressure is applied when cutting, even to a sharp saw, the consequences can be the same as described above.

So to the actual cutting. Although a line has been drawn right around the workpiece, you only need to follow two of these lines to make a square cut. Place the workpiece in a mitre block or on a bench hook to hold it steady while cutting.

When cutting the workpiece do not cut from the corner, **(PICTURE 6.45)** as this will mean that you will have to follow two cut lines. Carefully start the cut across the top of the workpiece, making sure the blade of the saw is accurately in line

6.45

with the marked line and just to the outside of the line so that you can see the line. **(PICTURE 6.46)** Then carefully cut down the side of the workpiece following the line marked.

6.46

Note: If you are cutting a wooden moulding, use a square and craft knife / scalpel before cutting to accurately score along the four drawn lines. The reason for doing this is so that when you cut the wood it will not leave a ragged edge.

13. HOW TO CORRECT A POORLY-CUT MITRE JOINT

The three main reasons for a poor mitre joint are that it is poorly cut; it is cut well but the corners of the room are not square; or a combination of both.

6.47

When the mitres have been cut and a test fit tried, only to find the joint is not acceptable, **(PICTURE 6.47)** the first thing to do is find out why. You will need to check both the mitre joint and the room to see if they are square.

6.48

Step A – check the mitre

First, see if the mitre is 90 degrees. Place the mitre together and check it with the square. Make sure that one length is along the blade of the square and the other along the stock. Now check that the two parts of the cornice are at 90 degrees to each other. **(PICTURE 6.48)** Check whether it a good joint, with no gaps where the mouldings meet.

Step B – check the room

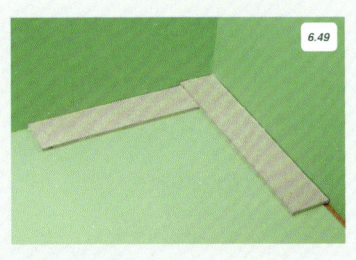

Now the corner of the room needs to be checked to see if it is square. The easiest way to do this is to make a template of the corner with two pieces of cardboard, superglue them together in the corner of the room with one strip along one wall, the other against the other wall. *(PICTURE 6.49)* Check this template to see if it is square as in step A.

Now that the mitre cut and the corner of the room have been checked you should know what is the cause of the problem. The technique to correct the problem is the same whichever of the three reasons is the cause: you will need to make a jig to place the mouldings in the correct position and fill the gap with car body filler.

Step C how to make the jig

Making the jig is very simple. All that is required is one piece of MDF as a base, and two strips of MDF to make the correct angle and to position the mouldings. *(PICTURE 6.50)*

Superglue one of the strips of MDF along one edge of the MDF base. *(PICTURE 6.51)* Place either the square or cardboard template (whichever is appropriate) up against the MDF that has just been glued down, then glue the other strip of MDF to the base up against the blade of the square *(PICTURE 6.52)* or edge of the cardboard template. *(PICTURE 6.53)* Take away the square or cardboard template. You then need to prepare the jig to correct the mouldings.

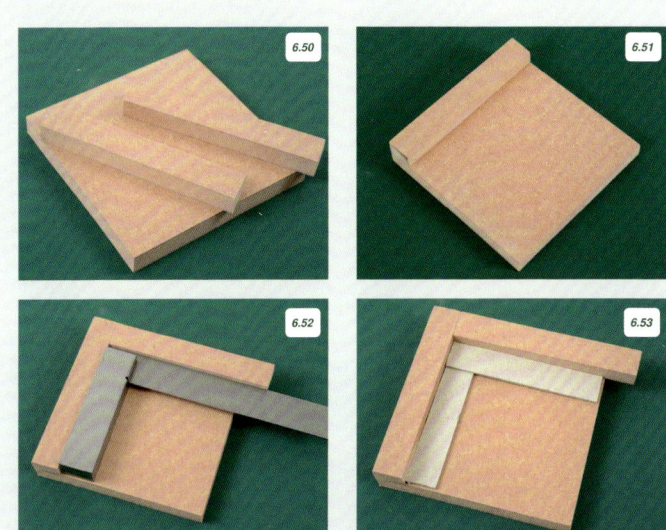

To prepare the jig to correct the moulding, a dam has to be built on the jig at the correct angle. To do this a line needs to be drawn on the base marking the position of the dam. If the jig was made using a square this line is drawn using a set square, this jig can be kept as it is a right angle and can be used for any square-cornered room. If the cardboard template was used then a line is drawn from the outside corner to the inside corner of the MDF, this jig is unlikely to be suitable for any other corner but do not discard as you never know. *(PICTURE 6.54)*

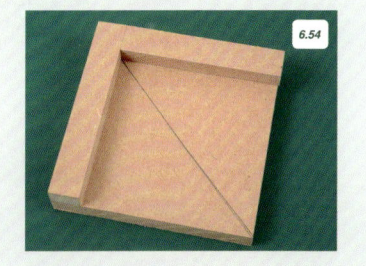

Along this line a piece of 1mm-thick styrene needs to be superglued. **(PICTURE 6.55)** This piece of styrene needs to be bigger than the ends of the mouldings that are to be corrected.

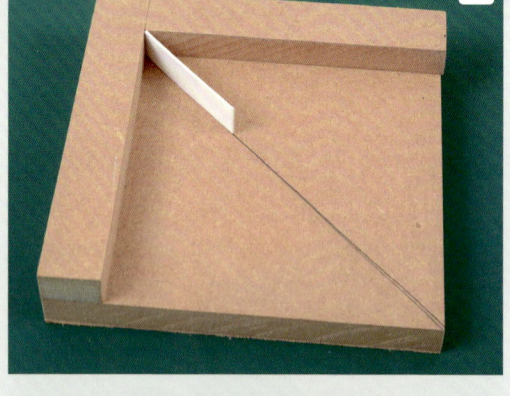

Now the jig and the dam need to have brown parcel tape placed where the filler will be, this will form a barrier so the filler will not stick to the dam or jig. **(PICTURE 6.56)** The reason to use parcel tape rather than clear tape is that you can see where the tape is.

Step D

Now that the jig is taped the mouldings can be corrected using car body filler. A small amount of filler is mixed (as per the 'manufacturers instructions). This filler is applied to the ends of the mouldings. **(PICTURE 6.57)**

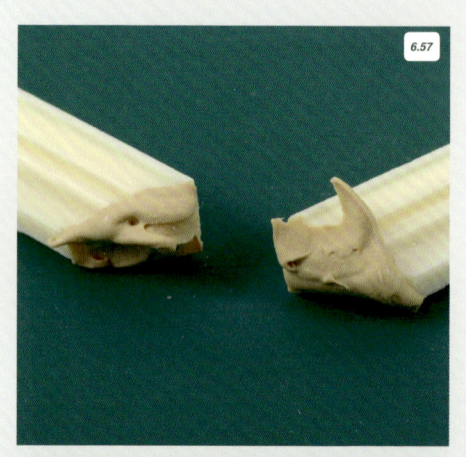

The mouldings are then pushed up against the dam, and any surplus filler will be squeezed out. With the moulding pushed tight up to the dam and up against the MDF sides they can be tacked in place with two drops of super glue. They can now be put aside until the filler has hardened. **(PICTURE 6.58)**

Step E – remove the jig

When the filler has completely hardened, the mouldings can be taken off the jig. First, using a craft knife / scalpel break the superglue fixing. The moulding will cleanly come away from the jig. Once the mouldings are free of the jig, use needle files and sanding sticks to shape the filler to the profile of the moulding. **(PICTURE 6.59)**

The mouldings should now make a perfect joint when fitted into the room. Place them into the corner to check that they fit.

14. SPRAYING

When spraying, the secret is not to rush and to use several light even coats. If you try to cover the item in one coat and the paint is sprayed on too heavily, the paint may collect in puddles, form runs and will even fill in fine detail.

Always keep the nozzle of the spray can at right angles to the item being sprayed. **(PICTURE 6.60)** Move the can left and right. Do not twist the can so that the nozzle points to one end of the workpiece then the other as this will result in a poor paint finish.

Words of warning:

- Always spray in a well-ventilated area
- Never spray anywhere near a naked flame or heat source
- Follow the instructions on the aerosol
- Wear a suitable face mask
- Wear disposable gloves
- Beware of overspray. Overspray, as the word suggests, is when the paint goes over the workpiece and lands everywhere. So if you are spraying on the antique dining table (not recommended), make sure it's well covered. The spray from an aerosol can covers a much wider area than you would think; so do make sure that enough newspaper has been laid out.

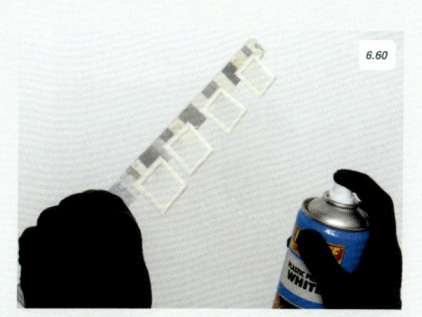

55

15. DECORATIVE PAINTING

Decorative painting is adding one or more colours to an item, as opposed to paint techniques such as weathering, wood graining etc. This is straightforward painting, but it may involve painting around some intricate detail or even a straight line. **(PICTURE 6.61)**

and household decorating paint or water-based paint such as tubes of artist's acrylic and household emulsion. Which one you use does not matter; it is a case of personal preference. However, beware of painting one on top of the other, as water and oil paints have different drying times. This can cause the topcoat of paint to crack (craze). This is a paint technique which is not wanted here.

Resin moulding can be painted in oil paint without priming, but if water-based paint is to be used, a resin moulding will need to be primed first, as resin has a smooth shiny surface. Two or three light coats of white car primer are all that is needed, then the resin moulding can be painted with either water or oil-based paint.

My preference is to use household emulsion paint, bought in tester pots available from all DIY shops. They are easy to use and come in a vast range of colours. **(PICTURE 6.62)**

There are no hard and fast rules to this very simple process, but for the best results very good paintbrushes are essential. Brushes are covered in chapter 1.

Paint is simply pigment (colour) suspended in a medium (either oil or water), giving you oil-based paint such as tubes of artist's oil paint

So now to the way I paint a moulding. I do not use the paint straight from the pot, as I like the paint to be thinner (more watery) than it comes in the tin. I have a small piece of polystyrene that I use as a palette. On this I mix a small amount of emulsion with water to the consistency that suits me. **(PICTURE 6.63)** As a rough guide, it's about two brush-loads of paint to one of water. I have never worked

case of applying thin coats of paint until I'm happy with the result. **(PICTURE 6.64)** Oil-based paints take a long time to dry, water-based paints are quick drying.

out an exact ratio of paint to water – I just add a bit more paint if it's too thin, or water if it's too thick, until I'm happy. The consistency of the paint is really a matter of personal preference.

I start by carefully painting around fine detail or straight lines with a number 0 paintbrush. The intention is not to paint the whole moulding with this brush, but to create a border that can be painted up to with a larger brush. The large areas can be filled in with a chisel brush.

The first coat will look streaky and thin. As with spraying, do not be tempted to try to paint the moulding in one coat. For the best finish, more light coats are better than one heavy one. I find that three light coats gives the moulding a solid colour, but you may need more coats of paint depending on the colour. For me it's a

16. HOW TO DE-TACK MASKING TAPE

De-tacking masking tape makes it less adhesive. This is useful for masking over paint so it does not take the paint off when the tape is removed. This technique is useful not only for masking over paint but for masking over any surface that needs a less aggressive adhesion. There are low-tack tapes on the market, but given the number of times that a low-tack tape is required I find it quicker to de-tack the tape myself.

There are two ways that I de-tack tape. The first is to hold a length of tape in one hand, then, using the other hand I run my finger and thumb down the tape two or three times. This will reduce the adhesion of the tape. **(PICTURE 6.65)**

The second way is to stick the tape to your clothing then peel it off and use it; this will have the same effect. **(PICTURE 6.66)**

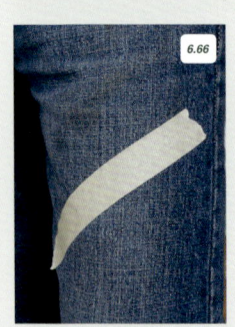

Always remove masking tape – de-tacked or not – slowly and carefully, looking all the time to see that nothing untoward is happening. Removing the tape quickly does not allow you to control any problem arising. If you see the tape is taking some of the underneath paint off, stop, then peel the tape off from the opposite direction. This can sometimes limit the damage.

17. HOW TO MAKE YOUR OWN TEMPLATES

This book has outlines of our ceiling panels, which can be used to make templates so you can make your own unique ceiling design. If you wish to create a design for walls, or incorporate another manufacturer's product into the design, then you will have to make your own templates.

The templates do not need to contain all the detail of the moulding; all that is necessary is that it is the correct size. Remember that you are making a design, not a detailed drawing of each and every one of the mouldings you wish to use.

The templates are there to block out the basic shape of each moulding in relation to each other, and as a group. This is to see if the design you want will fit into the space you have, to see if you like the design when it's finished and to calculate exactly how many mouldings are required.

All the information you really need is the height and width of the moulding. The depth of the moulding should not interfere with the design. This information should be on the manufacturer's website or in their catalogue. Miniature Mansions' website and catalogue has all this information, enabling you to make templates of any of our mouldings.

Most wall panels and other wall ornaments (such as door surrounds, pilasters or overmantels) are either squares or rectangles. Panels that are ornate or even curved will usually fit into one of these shapes.

Wall panel:

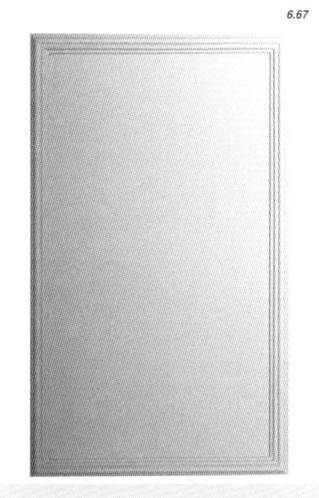

Let's start with a simple rectangular moulding SM30 Wall Panel. *(PICTURE 6.67)* You need to start with a right angle drawn onto a piece of cardboard to make a template. This is done using the set square. *(PICTURE 6.68)* This panel is $2^3/_8$" wide, so measuring off the vertical line, make two marks, one at the top and one at the bottom at $2^3/_8$", *(PICTURE 6.69)* then join up these marks. *(PICTURE 6.70)* As the panel is $3^{15}/_{16}$" high, and measuring this time from the horizontal line, repeat the above process, measuring to $3^{15}/_{16}$" and join the marks. *(PICTURE 6.71)* You then have the completed template ready to be cut out.

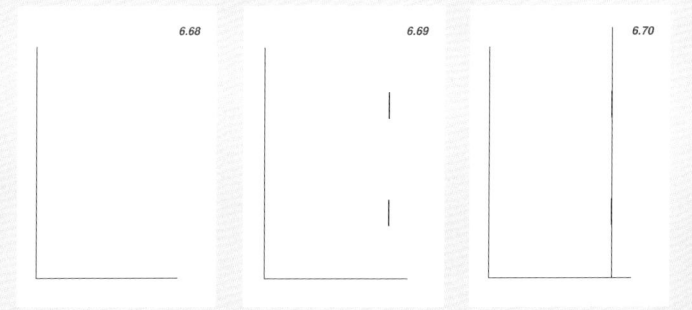

Before the template is cut out write on it the manufacturer's product code, what it is and the name of the manufacturer. *(PICTURE 6.72)*

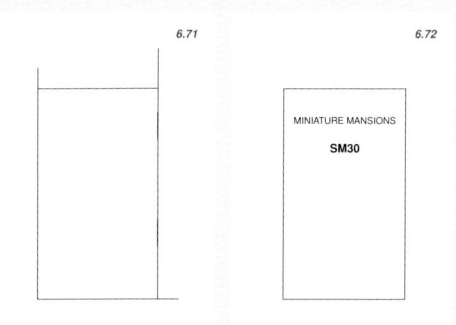

Door surround:

The next example is SM52 Door Surround. *(PICTURE 6.73)* Although this moulding has a lot of detail, all that is important for the design is the physical space the moulding will take up and not the detail or its exact shape. The overall size of the moulding is $4^{15}/_{16}$" wide by $8^3/_{16}$" high. The width of $4^{15}/_{16}$" is at the widest point which is the pediment at the top; there is no need to show that the body of the moulding is narrower than its widest point. Using the process

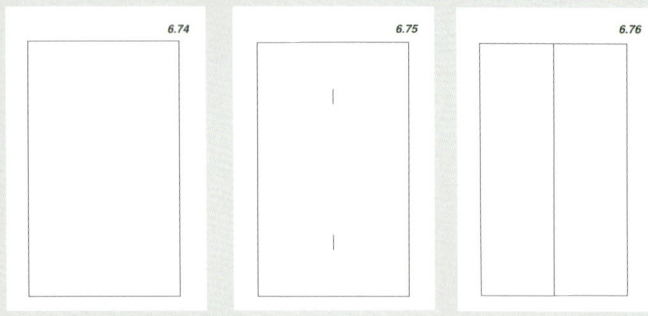

6.74

6.75

6.76

already described, draw a rectangle $4^{15}/_{16}$" wide by $8^{3}/_{16}$" high. **(PICTURE 6.74)**

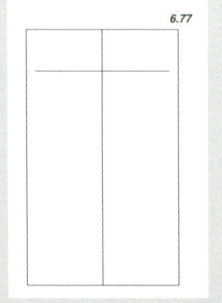

Mark out the door opening from a centre line. The centre line in this case is a line running from top to bottom down the middle of the template. Divide the width in two, which is $2^{15}/_{32}$" (for those who have forgotten how to divide a fractions of an inch, it is a simple matter of doubling the bottom number of the fraction so 16th becomes 32nd). From one edge of the rectangle, make two marks, one at the top and one at the bottom, $2^{15}/_{32}$" in. **(PICTURE 6.75)** These marks are joined to make the centre line. **(PICTURE 6.76)**

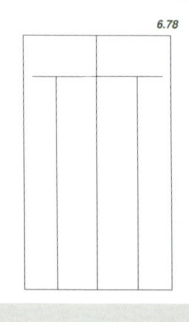

6.77

6.78

You can now draw the opening. The opening on this moulding is $2^{3}/_{4}$" wide by $6^{7}/_{8}$" high. From base line of the template, draw two marks $6^{7}/_{8}$", then join the marks to draw a line. **(PICTURE 6.77)** As with drawing the centre line, the opening width needs to be divided in two, so $2^{3}/_{4}$" becomes $1^{3}/_{8}$". Using the centre line to measure, mark and draw this distance on each side of the centre line. **(PICTURE 6.78)** Write the code number etc., then this template is ready to be cut out. The above process can be used to draw fire surrounds.

Arch:

The example this time is SM92 Arch. **(PICTURE 6.79)** This arch is $3^{1}/_{2}$" wide by $1^{7}/_{8}$" high with an opening of $2^{3}/_{4}$". Again, start by drawing a rectangle with a vertical centre line. **(PICTURE 6.80)** Set a compass from the centre line to the outside edge of the rectangle. Place the pencil point at the junction where the top line of the rectangle meets the centre line, and the point of the compass on the centre line, and then draw an arc. **(PICTURE 6.81)**

6.79

The opening is $2^{3}/_{4}$". Divide this by two, as before, to give $1^{3}/_{8}$". Measuring from the centre line, along the base line on one side, mark this measurement on the drawing. **(PICTURE 6.82)** Then set the compass from the centre line to this mark. Once set, place the point of the compass back on the point that the first arc was drawn from, and draw the inner arc. **(PICTURE 6.83)** The arch template is now ready to be cut out.

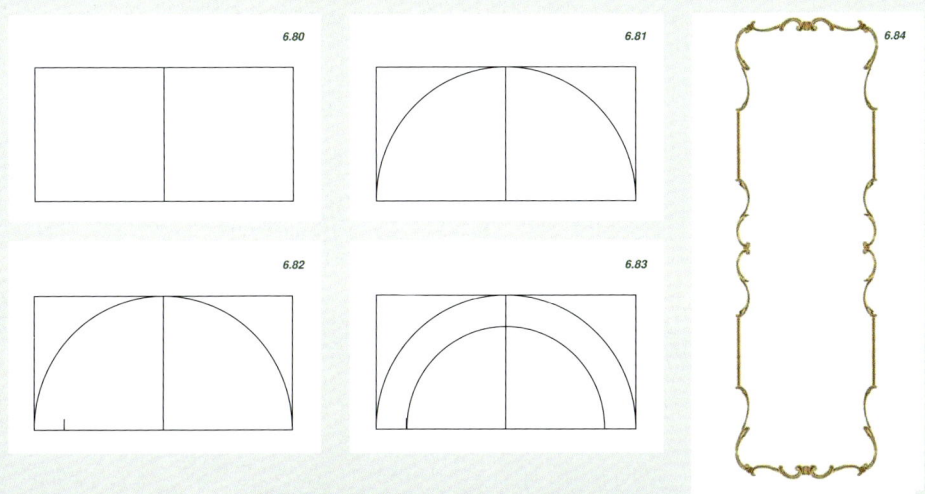

Template for a French-style wall panel

These panels are not in our range. **(PICTURE 6.84)** The curves need to be drawn with French curves. These are a set of three, multi-curved plastic shapes. (A more detailed description is the subject for another book.) For the design it is only the rectangular size that is really needed. So if you wish to have the curves, they can be drawn on free hand, once the correct size rectangle has been drawn.

61

TEMPLATES

SM121

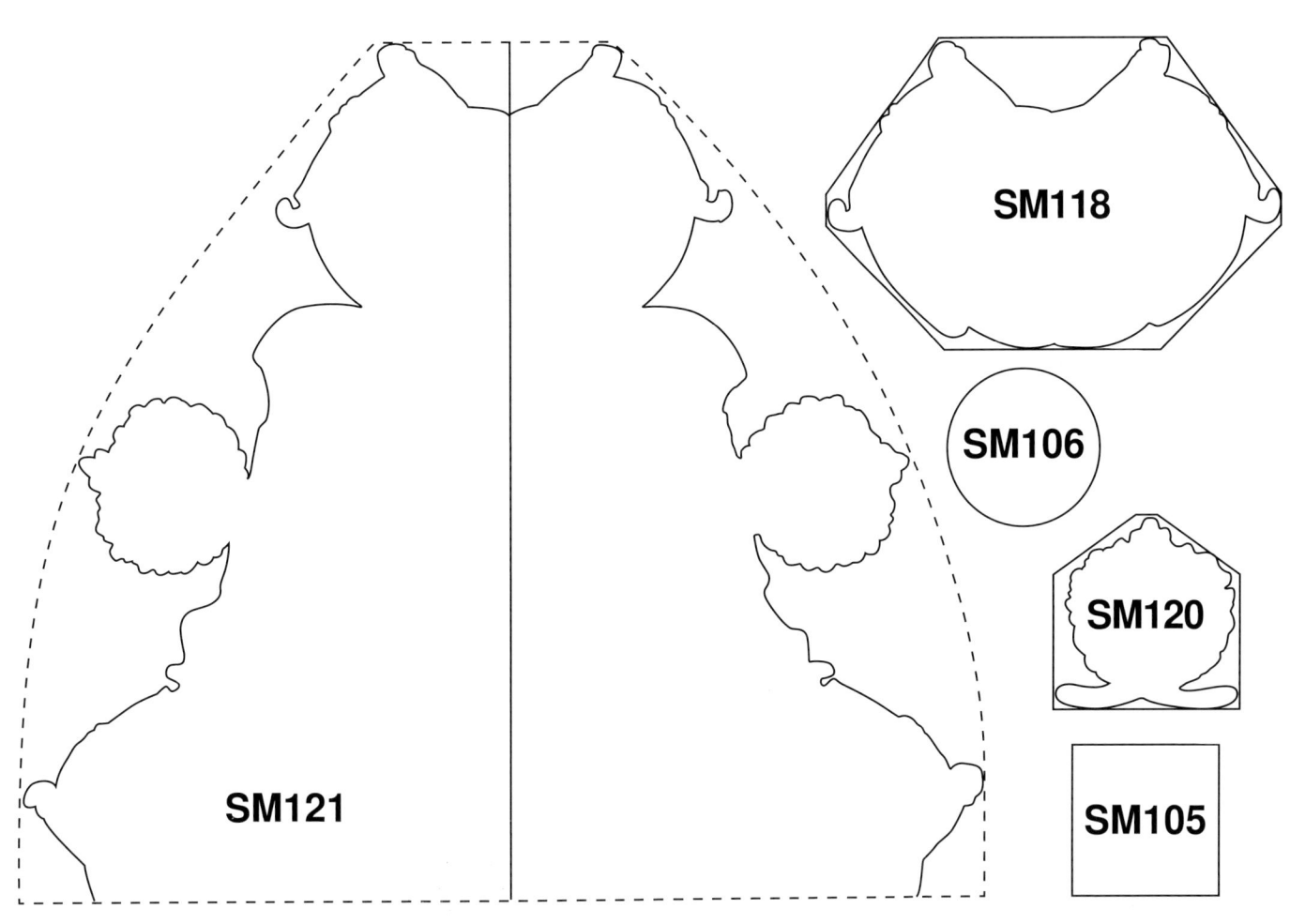

SM118

SM106

SM120

SM105

Copy twice as this is only half the moulding

SM35

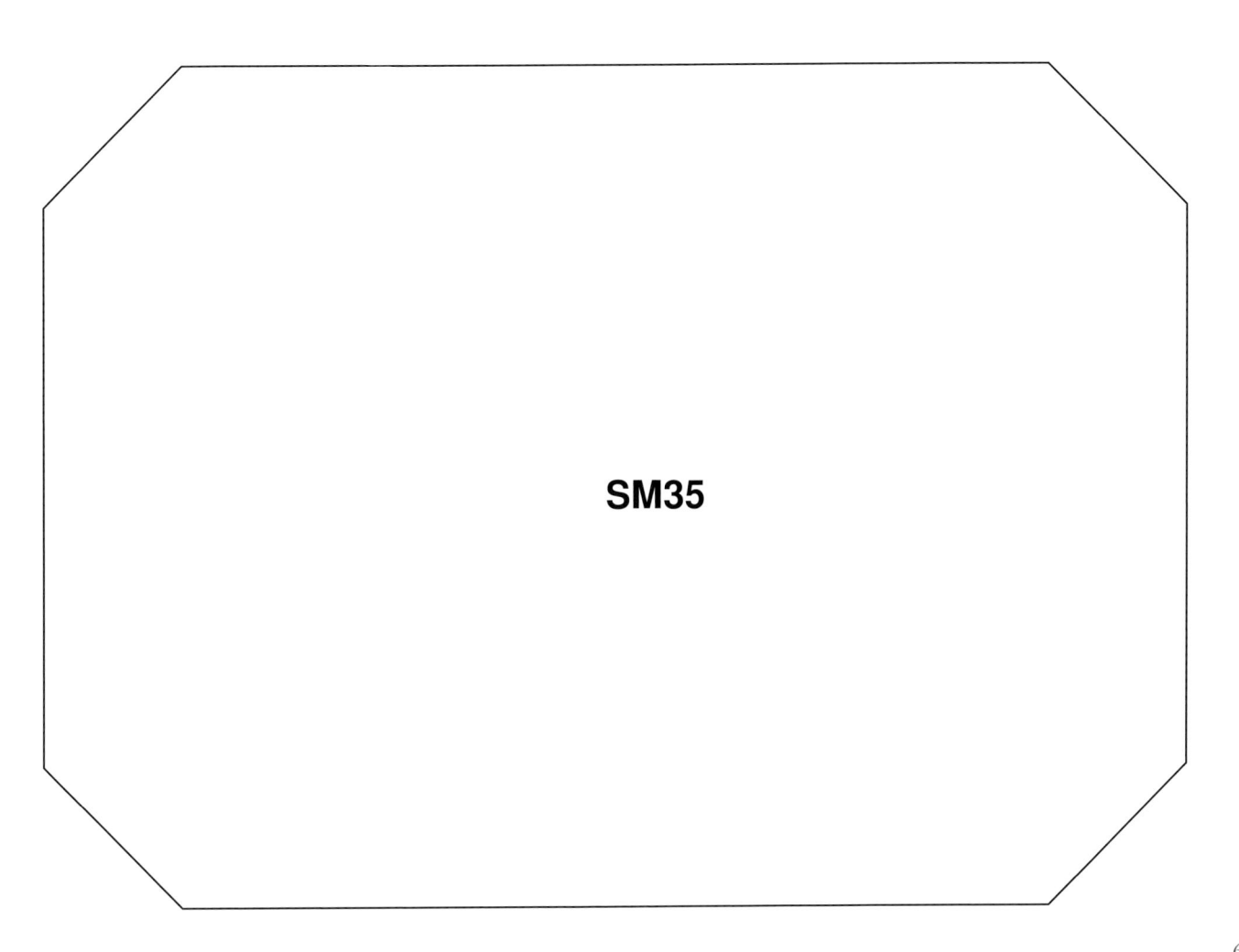

SM101 or SM111

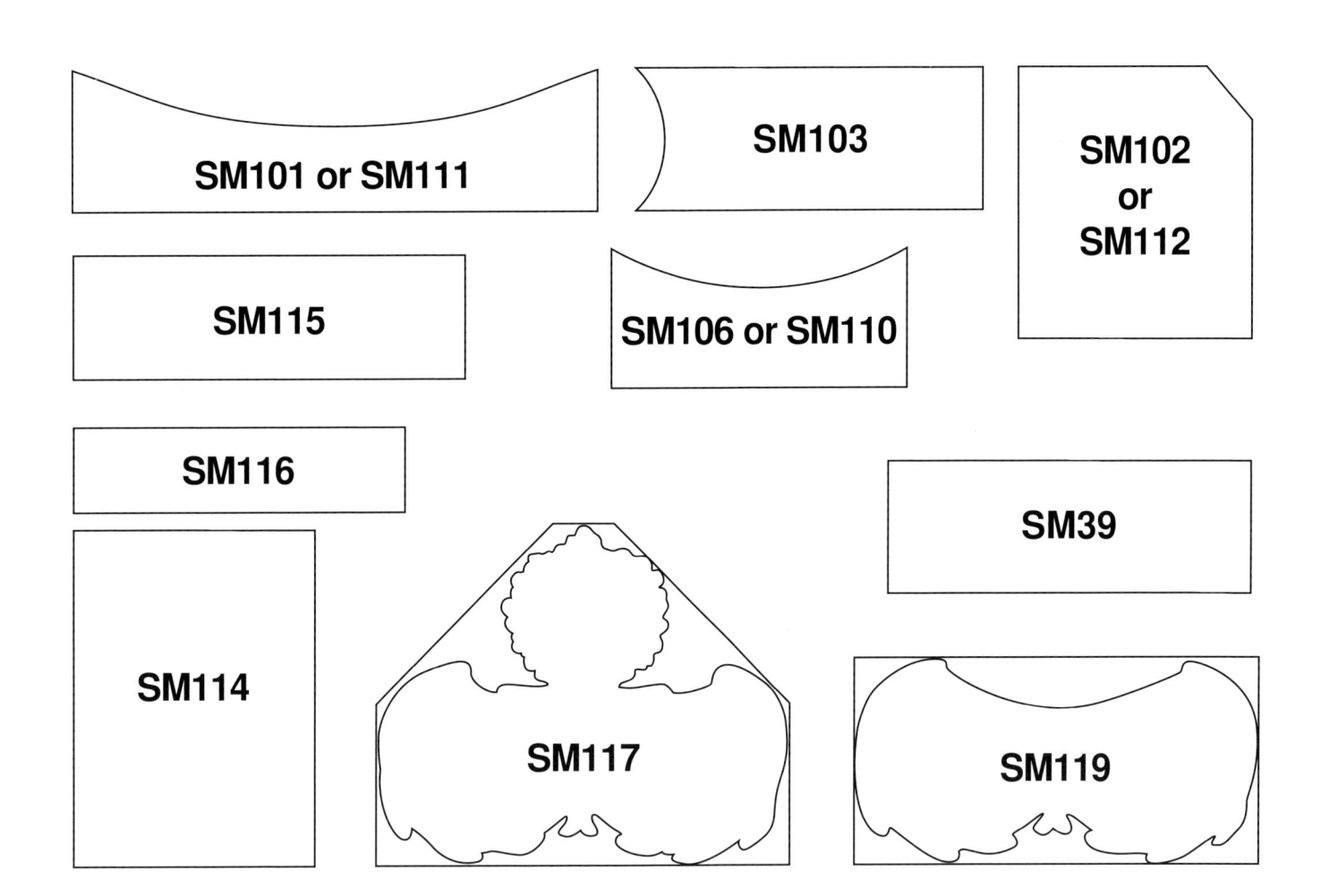

SM103

SM102 or SM112

SM115

SM106 or SM110

SM116

SM39

SM114

SM117

SM119

67

SM34

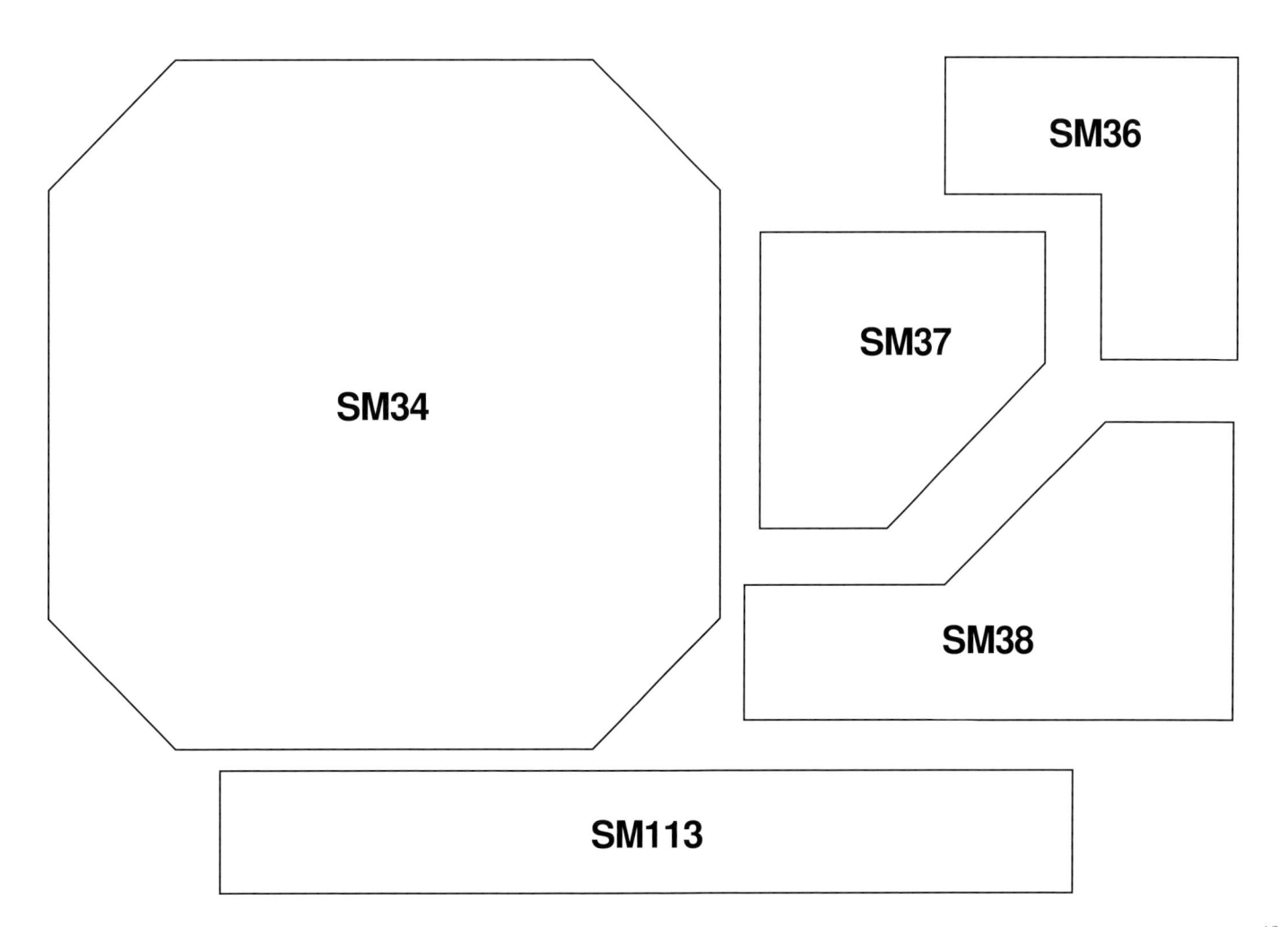

SM36

SM37

SM38

SM113

SM108

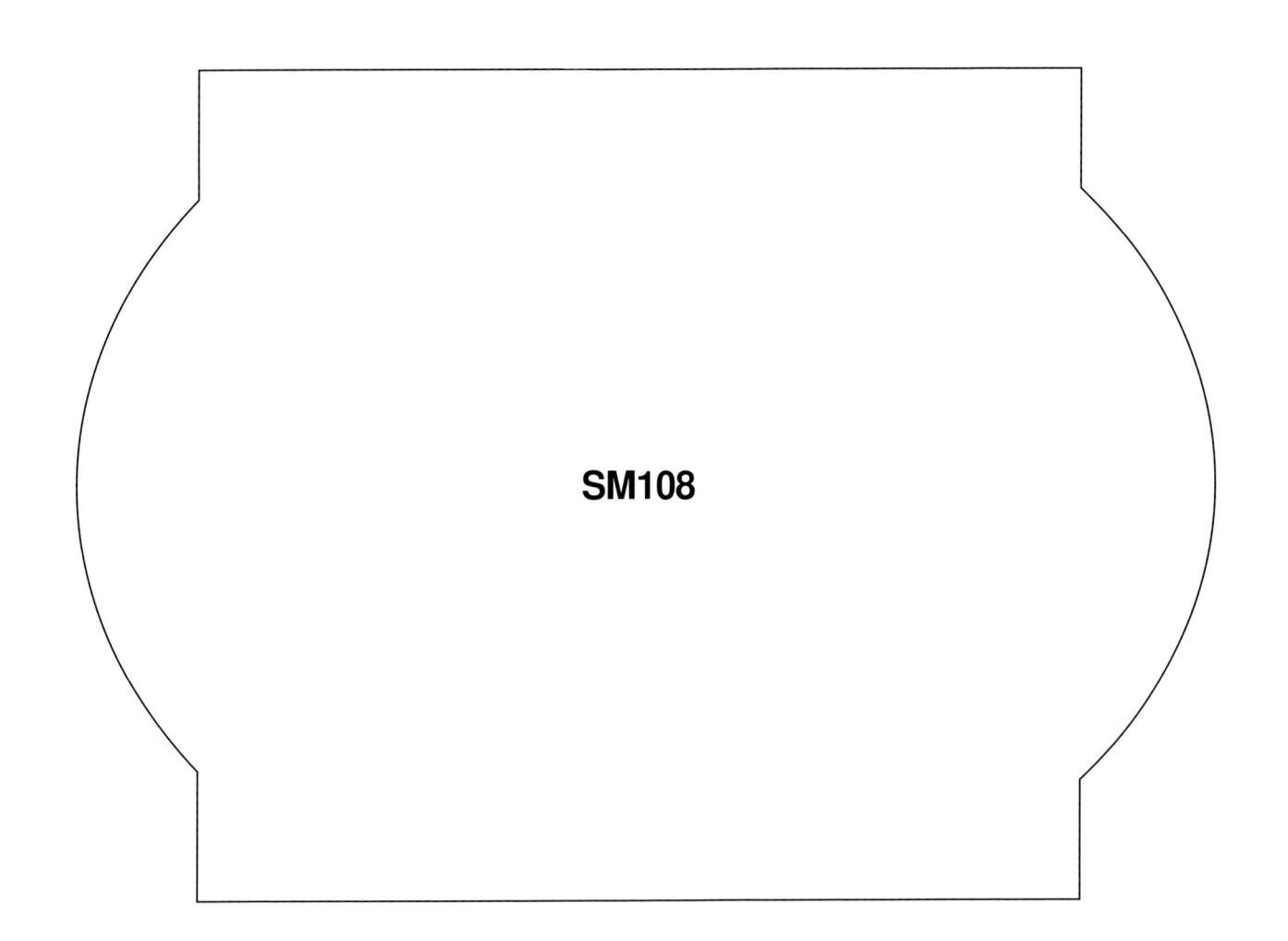

SM100 or SM107

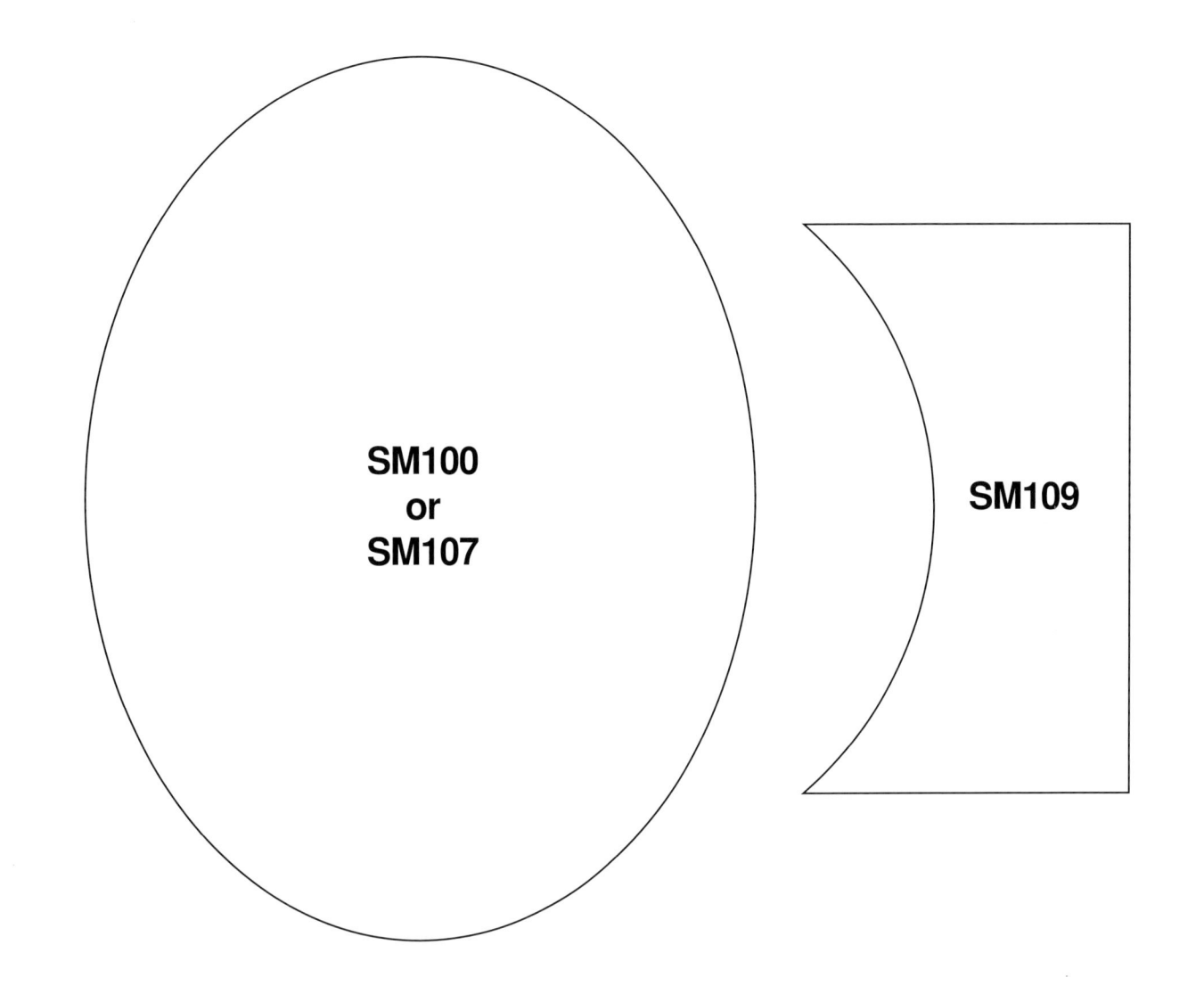

SM109